THE NEW
Students'
COOKBOOK

THE NEW Students' COOKBOOK

Carolyn Humphries

foulsham

LONDON • NEW YORK • TORONTO • SYDNEY

foulsham

The Oriel, Thames Valley Court, 183–187 Bath Road, Slough, Berkshire, SL1 4AA, England

Foulsham books can be found in all good bookshops and direct from www.foulsham.com

ISBN: 978-0-572-03521-1

Copyright © 2009 W. Foulsham & Co. Ltd

Cover photographs © Superstock and Istock

A CIP record for this book is available from the British Library

Printed in Great Britain by Printwise (Haverhill) Ltd, Haverill

Contents

Starting out   7

What you eat is important   9

Setting up your kitchen   11

Your first basic shop   13

Making the basics   15

And that means what?   19

Keeping it clean   21

Recipe notes   23

Really easy meals   25

Vegetarian meals   59

Chicken & turkey meals   93

Meat meals   111

Fish meals   149

Extra energy fodder   165

Simple desserts   173

Index   187

Starting out

You may never have had to cook for yourself before but it isn't that difficult and doesn't have to be expensive either. Eating takeaways every day isn't a sensible option. Not only will it cost you far too much but the poor nutrition will make you feel tired and sluggish and you're likely to get fat into the bargain!

This book won't insult you by telling you how to open a can of baked beans and put them on toast (mind you, that's a great standby when time and money are tight), but it does have plenty of tasty, nourishing meals that don't cost a fortune and

are easy and quick to make. It has advice on how to prepare and cook the basics such as vegetables, pasta, rice and eggs. It has simple ways to make meals go further if you decide to invite friends round, food to eat to keep you going during exams and tasty snacks that can easily turn into main meals to eke out the last of your cash. There's also a basic first shopping list to get you started and basic food hygiene advice. But it won't tell you to keep your room tidy or remind you to do your washing and ironing – that's up to you!

What you eat is important

To enjoy life to the full (and to help the brain cells work), a healthy diet is vital. You need a balance made up of the following food groups:

- At least five portions of **fruit and vegetables** a day (that doesn't include potatoes). You need them for vitamins, minerals, fibre and general well-being. Many are also cheap, which helps a lot. Eat them cooked or raw, canned, frozen or fresh.

TIP: Market stalls are likely to be cheaper than the supermarket for fresh produce. If you are buying in a supermarket look for economy ranges or buy loose rather than pre-packed – it's cheaper.

- Loads of **starchy foods** (complex carbohydrates) for energy and to fill you up. At least half of what you eat should come from bread, potatoes, rice, pasta and breakfast cereals (wholegrain varieties such as muesli, porridge oats, Weetabix or Shredded Wheat rather than sugary ones). They provide slow-release energy to keep you sustained both in body and mind!

TIP: Buy supermarket own brands – they're much cheaper.

- At least two portions of **protein** a day for body growth and repair. Best found in meat, poultry, fish, eggs, dairy products such as cheese, milk and yoghurt, pulses (dried peas, beans and lentils, including baked beans in tomato sauce) and vegetable protein such as tofu, TVP (like dried soya mince) and Quorn. Avocados and bananas are also good sources.

TIP: Cheap cuts of meat are just as good for you as expensive ones and all species of fish are equally nutritious, regardless of cost. But if you go for economy ranges of, say, sausages, they are likely to contain a lot of rusk filler and be fattier with less actual meat than a good quality one. Read the labels to be sure what you are buying. You will probably enjoy them more and feel just as full after two good sausages as four economy ones – and they're better for you!

- A **very little fat** – essential for body warmth and energy, BUT you don't need masses of extra butter or margarine or loads of oil for frying. You get most of what you need naturally in other foods, such as dairy products, meat and cereals, so have only a scraping of butter or margarine on bread, use the minimum amount of oil for cooking (drain well before eating) and grill rather than deep-fry foods where possible.

TIP: Avoid too many takeaways and ready meals. Not only are they expensive, they're also high in fat, salt and sugar.

Setting up your kitchen

Most furnished accommodation supplies basic kitchen equipment. All being well this will include a cooker with an oven and a fridge with either a freezer or freezing compartment. Most students need to take their own crockery and cutlery, tea towels and washing up cloths.

For cooking utensils, you don't need much and you certainly don't need expensive gadgets.

- Bowls – including one that's microwave safe and big enough for mixing as well as jobs like scrambling eggs
- Chopping board
- Colander or large sieve for straining cooked vegetables, pasta or rice
- Draining spoon, long-handled, with holes in it
- Fish slice for lifting foods out of a frying pan or from a baking sheet
- Frying pan
- Grater
- Kettle and toaster (You could wait until you get to where you're staying as you may find everyone else has them)
- Kitchen scissors
- Knives – vegetable knife, cook's knife (for cutting meat) and bread knife
- Oven gloves
- Ovenproof dish
- Paperware – kitchen paper, foil and/or cling film
- Potato masher (use a fork if you don't have one)
- Potato peeler (easier than a vegetable knife)
- Roasting tins
- Saucepans, ideally one small, one medium and one large, with lids
- Whisk – a balloon or wire one is ideal for making sauces etc.
- Wooden spoon

Your first basic shop

If you're lucky, your parents will be keen to buy a box of essentials to take with you (so they know you can survive the first few days). If you give them this list, it'll help with ideas for the basics for everyday life and a few of the mainstay store cupboard ingredients you'll often need for cooking the recipes in this book.

Basic cupboard fodder

- Cereal – wholegrain is better than sugary; it'll fill you up and give you energy for longer

- Curry powder or curry paste

- Garlic – a tub or jar is much easier than fiddling around crushing cloves – store in the fridge once opened

- Herbs – dried mixed herbs are good for flavouring lots of savoury dishes but if you are more adventurous you might add dried oregano, basil, mint, and sage

- Honey – good for sweetening and on toast

- Marmalade, jam and Marmite (or other yeast extract) for toast

- Mayonnaise or salad cream

- Milk powder or long life milk – for when you run out of fresh

- Oil – sunflower, vegetable or olive

- Parmesan-style cheese – a tub of dried, grated Italian hard cheese

- Pasta

- Plain flour (and self-raising if you plan to do any baking)

- Raisins or sultanas – good for snacking, on cereals and in lots of recipes

- Rice – long grain

- Salt and pepper – preferably buy a mill filled with black peppercorns

- Sauces – tomato ketchup, brown, Worcestershire and soy sauces

- Spices – chilli powder and ground cinnamon to start

- Stock cubes – vegetable and/or chicken

- Sugar – caster is fine for most uses

- Tea and coffee

- Tomato purée – a tube is easiest – store in fridge once opened

- Vinegar – white wine will do for anything

Cans

- Tomatoes – economy brands are fine, and whole are cheaper than ready chopped (just crush up with a wooden spoon when you add them)
- Baked beans
- Red kidney beans
- Sweetcorn
- Tuna – supermarkets have low-price cans alongside the famous brands (they should now all carry the 'dolphin-friendly' symbol)

In the fridge

- Bread – it'll keep longer in the fridge
- Butter or margarine
- Cheddar cheese – choose a strong flavoured one, if you like it, then you don't need to use so much in cooking
- Eggs
- Milk – keep a carton in the freezer so you won't run out; it does take ages to thaw though, and will need a good shake once defrosted

Making the basics

The old expression 'He can't even boil an egg' isn't so funny – many people can't! Here are some simple instructions for all the basic foods you'll want to cook.

TIP An egg pricker, which you can buy in hardware shops, is a great little gadget. You pierce the air sac end of the egg and it prevents it cracking when boiling.

Eggs

Boiled: Place the eggs in a small saucepan and just cover with cold water. Cover with a lid (for quicker boiling) and bring to the boil. As soon as the water boils, start your timer and cook for $3\frac{1}{2}$ minutes for runny yolks and firm whites, 5–6 minutes for hard-boiled.

TIP For hard-boiled eggs to eat cold, plunge them immediately into cold water after cooking and shell them quickly to stop that black ring forming round the yolks.

Fried: Heat a very little oil in a frying pan. Break each egg into a cup and slide gently into the hot oil. Spoon a little oil over the eggs as they fry and remove with a fish slice as soon as they are cooked how you like them.

Poached: Bring a frying pan of water to the boil and then turn down the heat until there are just tiny bubbles. Add 1 tbsp of vinegar or lemon juice. Break each egg into a cup, then gently slide into the simmering water. Cook for 3 minutes for soft yolks, 4–5 minutes for hard. Do not boil rapidly or the white will break up. Lift out with a fish slice. Use very fresh eggs.

Scrambled: Heat a knob of butter or margarine and 1 tbsp of milk for each egg in a saucepan. Whisk in the eggs with a whisk or a fork. When well blended, add a little salt and pepper and cook over a gentle heat, stirring all the time until the mixture scrambles but is still creamy. Do not allow to boil or it will go rubbery and watery. Serve immediately and soak the pan in hot soapy water straight away or it will be horrible to clean!

Omelette: See page 41.

Potatoes

Boiled: Peel or scrub and cut into even-sized pieces. Place in a pan with just enough cold water to cover. Add a pinch of salt, if you like. Part-cover with a lid, bring to the boil, reduce the heat slightly and boil quickly until tender (about 10 minutes, depending on the size of the pieces). Drain.

TIP When a sharp knife slides easily into the potatoes, they are ready.

Chips: Oven chips are the easiest option, and to save fuel you can also cook them in the grill pan under a moderate grill instead of in the oven, but do keep turning them and watch carefully as they burn easily. Not quite the same as the real thing, though, so here's how it's done.

Peel, if you like, and cut each potato into finger-thick slices. Then cut each slice into chips. Pat dry on kitchen paper or on a clean tea towel. Heat enough oil to three-quarters fill the frying pan, or at least 2.5 cm in a saucepan (or use a chip pan if you have one). To test the temperature, slide in one chip down the back of the fish slice into the oil. If it starts to sizzle immediately, the oil is ready. Gently slide the chips down the fish slice into the pan a handful at a time, and spread them out with the slice. Cook until golden and soft in the centre. Drain on kitchen paper before serving.

TIP Don't add more chips than the pan will hold comfortably – if they are packed in and sticking out of the oil the temperature will drop too much and they will stew rather than fry crisply. Better to cook two batches if necessary.

Jacket-baked: Scrub, leave whole and prick a few times with a fork. Rub with oil and salt (if you like) and place directly on the middle shelf of the oven. Bake at 180°C/350°F/gas 4/fan oven 160°C for about 1 hour or until the potatoes feel soft when squeezed with an oven-gloved hand. The oven temperature isn't vital; cook for longer in a slower oven or for less time in a hotter oven.

TIP If you thread the potatoes on to metal skewers they will cook more quickly. Don't put on an oven for just one or two potatoes – it's a waste of fuel, for which read money.

If you have a microwave, prick the potatoes, wrap in kitchen paper and microwave for about 4 minutes per potato until soft when squeezed. Leave to stand for a few minutes before eating. They taste better if you crisp the skins under a hot grill for a few minutes.

Mashed: Peel first and prepare as for boiled. Once cooked and drained, add a knob of butter or margarine and a dash of milk. Mash with a potato masher or fork until smooth, then beat briefly until fluffy. You can add a little more milk or butter if it doesn't look creamy enough.

Roast: Peel or scrub and cut into even-sized pieces. Place in a pan and just cover with water. Add a pinch of salt, part-cover with a lid, bring to the boil and cook for about 3 minutes. Drain off the water. Cover firmly with the lid and, holding the lid on, give the pan a really good shake to roughen the edges of the potatoes. Meanwhile, heat a little oil in a roasting tin in the oven at 190°C/375°F/gas 5/fan oven 170°C until sizzling. Add the potatoes (careful – they will spit). Turn over in the oil then roast at the top of the oven for about 1 hour, turning once or twice during the cooking time, until crisp and golden.

Sautéed: Cut into small pieces or dice. Heat a little oil (or half butter or margarine, half oil) in a frying pan and fry, turning, until golden brown and cooked through – about 7 minutes, depending on the size. Add a little garlic towards the end of cooking, if you like. Drain on kitchen paper before serving.

TIP *Courgettes are great cooked this way too and they'll cook a bit quicker.*

Carrots and other root vegetables

Boiled: Peel or scrub, then slice or cut into fingers. Place in a pan with just enough cold water to cover. Add a pinch of salt, if you like. Part-cover with a lid, bring to the boil, reduce the heat slightly and boil quickly until just tender (about 6 minutes, depending on the size of the pieces). Drain.

Roast: Peel and cut in even-sized pieces. No need to par-boil them unless you're cooking potatoes too. Toss in oil in a baking tin and roast as for potatoes.

Green vegetables

Boiled: Shred or tear leafy ones; separate broccoli or cauliflower into small florets; top and tail beans or mangetout; top, tail and slice runner beans; shell peas or broad beans. Bring a little lightly salted water to the boil, add the vegetables, push down in the boiling water, cover and boil rapidly until just tender, no longer – usually just a few minutes. Drain (use the liquid for gravy or sauce) and serve.

Steamed: Prepare your veg as above but place in a metal colander over a pan of boiling water. Cover with a lid and steam until just tender – just 5–8 minutes. Don't put too many in the colander at one time, spread out evenly and allow a little longer than for boiling. Don't overcook or they will lose their colour and nutrients.

Frozen veg: Peas are a great standby but bags of loose frozen veg – broccoli, cauliflower – also save waste and help you get your five a day. Microwave in a shallow dish with 2 tbsp water or tip them frozen into a pan of rapidly boiling water, turn the heat up high to bring back to the boil, then boil for a couple of minutes until just tender.

Vegetables – and other things

Stir-fried: This is a way of cooking vegetables – and other ingredients – quickly so they stay crunchy and delicious. Cut into thin strips as near the same size as possible so they cook evenly. Heat a little oil in a wok or frying pan until really hot. If using meat or poultry, add first and stir all the time for a couple of minutes before adding vegetables, then add these and continue to stir over a high heat, so they mix and cook evenly, for a few minutes until cooked to your liking. The vegetables should still be slightly crunchy.

Rice

Boiled: Rinse and drain the rice. Bring a large pan of lightly salted water to the boil, add the rice, stir, then boil rapidly for 10 minutes or according to packet directions until the rice is tender but the grains are still separate. Strain in a colander and pour some boiling water over to rinse off any excess starch, then drain again.

TIP *One serving is about 2 handfuls or 1/4 mug of uncooked rice.*

Oven-baked: Use 1 measure of rice and 2½ times as much salted water or stock, so for 4 people, use a mug of rice and 2½ mugs of liquid. Melt a knob of butter or margarine in a flameproof dish, then stir in the rice. Add the stock or water and bring to the boil. Cover with foil or a lid and place in the oven at 180°C/350°F/gas 4/fan oven 160°C. Cook for 20 minutes or until the rice is tender and has absorbed all the liquid. Don't overcook or it will go mushy.

TIP Ovenproof means it goes in the oven – like Pyrex – flameproof means you can use it on the hob. If in doubt, use a saucepan on the hob.

Steamed: Use the same quantities as for oven-baked rice. Rinse the rice and put it in a pan. Cover with the liquid and bring just to the boil. Cover with a piece of foil, then a tight fitting lid. Turn down the heat as low as possible and cook for 15 minutes. Keep the lid on. Turn off the heat and leave to stand for 5 minutes (no more), then remove the cover and fluff up with a fork.

Pasta

Bring plenty of lightly salted water to the boil. Add the pasta and bring back to the boil. Add 1 tbsp oil to prevent it boiling over, then boil rapidly uncovered for about 10 minutes or according to packet directions, stirring occasionally to prevent sticking, until the pasta is just tender but still with a little 'bite'. Drain.

TIP Allow 2 large handfuls of uncooked pasta shapes per person, 3 if they are large shapes, or ⅙–¼ x 500 g packet spaghetti (depending on appetites). For spaghetti, bring the water to the boil, then stand the spaghetti in the water and gently push down so the spaghetti curls round in the pan as it softens in the boiling water.

And that means what?

Once you start to get interested in cooking and you look at more recipes, you'll come across cookery terms that may be unfamiliar. If you haven't come across them watching Gordon or Jamie, here's what they mean.

Beat: Tilt the bowl of ingredients in one hand and stir round fast and firmly in one direction with a wooden spoon. Keep going until it's smooth.

TIP To chop fresh herbs, put them in a mug and snip with scissors.

Chop: Cut any vegetable or fruit in half first so the flat cut side is down on the chopping board. Then hold firmly in one hand and, using a sharp knife, make cuts at even distances along the length of the food not quite through one end. Then, still holding it together, make cuts across it so that it is cut into small pieces. To chop finely, simply make the cuts closer together; to chop coarsely … you don't need me to tell you.

TIP If you hate chopping onions, buy a bag of frozen, diced onion and use a handful instead.

Dice: Much like chopping but into bigger cubes and you can cut right through the food at both ends as it's easier to hold together.

Flameproof: This is not the same as 'ovenproof' but means anything that can go on the hob or under the grill. If in doubt about a casserole dish that you want to use under the grill, for example – don't.

Fold: This is like mixing lightly to keep air in a mixture. Use a metal spoon and gently cut and turn over the mixture using a figure-of-eight motion.

Grate: Hold the grater firmly in one hand over a plate and rub the ingredient to be grated up and down the appropriate side of the grater. Use the different sides to grate coarsely for cheese, carrots or chocolate, medium for lemon rind, or finely for nutmeg.

Knead: Gently work the mixture – usually dough – together to a ball with your hands, then put it on a board and squeeze and press until it forms a ball without any cracks. For bread, you hold it with one hand, use the heel of the other to stretch the dough away from you then fold it back over itself and keep repeating the process until it is smooth and elastic.

Mash: Use a potato masher or fork. Press the ingredient against the sides and base of the bowl or pan so it is forced through the gaps in the fork or masher to form a smoothish paste.

TIP *For potatoes or other cooked veg add a knob of butter or margarine and give them a good beat with the masher or a wooden spoon once mashed to make them fluffy.*

Pare: Cut thin shreds of rind off something with a small, sharp knife.

Ovenproof: Not surprisingly, a dish or pan that can go in the oven. Pyrex is fine. Watch out for Bakelite handles on any of your pans; they are not ovenproof. This is not the same as 'flameproof'.

Roll: Dust the work surface with flour to stop it sticking and roll the pastry or dough firmly but evenly with a rolling pin (or clean milk or wine bottle), always rolling away from you. Give the dough a quarter turn and repeat.

TIP *Don't roll from side to side as it stretches the dough, which will then shrink when you cook it.*

Slice into rings: To slice an onion into rings, don't bother to peel it, just cut it across in slices the thickness you want, then remove the outer two layers and separate the rest into rings. Discard the ends.

Separate an egg: The easiest way is to break the egg on to a saucer. Then hold an egg cup or half the egg shell over the yolk and strain the white into a separate container.

Whip/whisk: Use a balloon whisk to beat the mixture in a circular motion, making sure you lift the mixture up with the whisk as you go to incorporate as much air as possible.

Keeping it clean

This is all pretty much common sense but if you – or any of your housemates – are not strong in that suit, it's worth reminding yourselves of some basic kitchen hygiene to avoid any unpleasant side effects!

In the kitchen

- Wash your hands before you start cooking – you know where they've been

- Clean the work surface before you cook – how clean were your mate's jeans when he sat on it last night?

- Wipe up spills as they happen – and before they go hard and crusty

- Use a clean cloth – otherwise you'll wipe more germs around

- Wash up sooner rather than later – the longer you leave it, the harder it'll be

- Wash up in hot, soapy water (if you wear much-maligned Marigolds, you can put your hands in hot water) – it's much easier!

- Leave to drain rather than dry up with a grubby tea towel – enough said

- Sweep up – food bits on the floor attract mice ... and other nasties

- Empty rubbish as soon as the bin is full – if it spills on the floor or the bag splits, that's more clearing up ... or mice

Storing food

- Keep an eye on the use-by date and use it up

- If you buy things cheaply on their sell-by date – a good way to save – use them by the use-by date or freeze them immediately

- Don't refreeze anything unless you cook it first – check the labels to make sure chilled food has not been frozen. Fish, in particular, sold in chill cabinets has often been previously frozen.

- Thaw frozen foods thoroughly – overnight in the fridge is best – and use straight away

- Wrap perishables and keep them in the fridge

- Don't put cans in the fridge – move half-used canned food to a container with a lid

- Don't leave cooked food lying around – it's a perfect breeding ground for bacteria, not to mention a feeding ground for mice

- Cool leftovers quickly by transferring them from their hot container into a clean cold one. Cover loosely and as soon as they're properly cold, cover and put in the fridge

- Wrap raw meat or fish well and keep it on the bottom shelf in the fridge where it can't drip on anything. Don't mix raw and cooked meats or fish on the same shelf

- Don't keep food festering in the fridge – taste and smell are often a good guide to the state of your food: anything that looks, smells or tastes off, is off!

When you are cooking

- Thaw frozen meat thoroughly before cooking, especially poultry

- Check instructions on prepared frozen foods to see if they should be cooked from frozen or thawed first

- Try to resist licking your fingers then continuing to cook

- Don't keep tasting and stirring with the same spoon; use a clean spoon to taste

- Check any food is thoroughly cooked through before serving

- Make sure reheated food is piping hot right through – eat it lukewarm and you're asking for trouble

- Don't reheat foods more than once

Recipe notes

● I've used an average sized mug to measure ingredients – or if you get some cup measures from a kitchen shop, use them. A mug should be only loosely packed in to the level you would fill if making a drink– not crammed full. See the chart below for approximate metric equivalents in case you want to measure using scales.

1 mug = 250 ml liquid

= 100 g shelled or diced fresh or frozen veg, such as peas

= 100 g flour and bulgar (cracked wheat)

= 175 g couscous and lentils

= 225 g sugar, rice, butter or margarine

● All spoon measures are level: 1 tsp = about 5 ml, 1 tbsp = about 15 ml

● All eggs are medium unless otherwise stated

● All can sizes are approximate – they differ slightly from brand to brand but not by enough to make a difference so, for instance, if a recipe calls for a 400 g can and yours is 425 g, that's fine

● Wash and peel, if necessary, all fresh produce before using

● All preparation and cooking times are approximate

● Always preheat the oven and cook on the centre shelf unless otherwise stated (not so important if you have a fan oven)

● Some recipes serve at least two people, so if you're eating alone have it on two days. You can in most cases halve the quantities if you like, but it's just as quick to cook enough for two meals in one go!

Really easy meals

If you are an absolute beginner, really pushed for time, or want a light lunch or something before you go out, there's loads of choice here – or you can add extra salad, bread or a jacket potato to make a more substantial meal.

Stuffed jacket potatoes

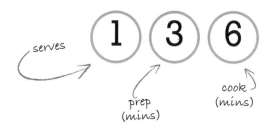

serves

1 3 6

prep (mins)

cook (mins)

Here are some ideas to spice up that great standby the jacket potato. If you are not cooking anything else in the oven, cook it by the microwave method, then flash it under the grill to crisp the skin. The cooking time is based on that.

1 jacket potato – as big as you like – and as much filling as you want!

1 Cook the potato as described on page 16.

2 Split the potato in half. Mash in a little butter or margarine (and a dash of Marmite, or other yeast extract, if you love it) then top with any of these:

- Baked beans (hot or cold) and grated cheese

- Chopped ham and chopped peppers

- Grated Cheddar cheese or crumbled blue cheese

- Sweetcorn (hot or cold) and grated cheese

- Tuna, chopped cucumber and mayonnaise

- Chopped grilled bacon

- A few prawns mixed with mayonnaise and a squirt of tomato purée

Pasta with ...

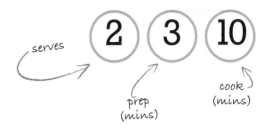

Pasta is bound to turn up pretty often in your cooking. The purists would disagree, but in a student kitchen, you can use any pasta for any dish. Generally, a thicker sauce complements a chunkier pasta.

About 2 good handfuls of <u>pasta</u> per person, plus your sauce

1 Cook the pasta as described on page 18.

2 Drain the cooked pasta, then return it to the pan and stir in any of these until piping hot:

- Chopped canned tomatoes, a few dried herbs and grated cheese

- Drained canned peas, some crème fraîche, a pinch of dried mint, seasoned to taste

- Egg beaten with a little milk, salt and pepper, a few mixed herbs and/or grated cheese

- Egg beaten with a little milk, seasoning and some drained canned sweetcorn and/or tuna

- Knob of butter or margarine and grated cheese

- Knob of butter or margarine, a small spoonful of Marmite, or other yeast extract, and grated cheese

- Peanut butter, a little milk and a pinch of chilli powder, with cheese too, if you like

- Spoonful of pesto sauce

Easy rice meals

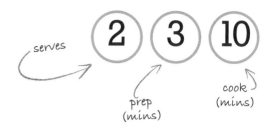

serves

2 3 10

prep (mins)

cook (mins)

Here are some ideas to spice up plain boiled rice to make a tasty meal. It's another good thing to have in your cupboard. Different types will take different times to cook so glance at the packet directions before you start.

2 good handfuls of <u>rice</u> per person, plus your flavourings

1 Cook the rice as described on pages 17–18.

2 Drain the cooked rice, then return it to the pan and stir in any of the following until hot:

- Chopped can of tomatoes, some dried herbs and diced ham or salami, topped with grated Parmesan

- Cooked frozen peas, a beaten egg and some soy or Worcestershire sauce

- Drained can of pineapple, a drained can of butter beans (or other pulses) or some diced tofu and mayonnaise or soy sauce (good hot or cold)

- Drained can of tuna, some raisins or sultanas, diced cucumber and some mayonnaise, flavoured with a little curry powder, if liked (good hot or cold)

- Drained canned red kidney beans, a pinch of chilli powder, dried oregano and some grated cheese

    Or take a look in the cupboard or fridge and experiment with what's there.

Thick mixed vegetable soup

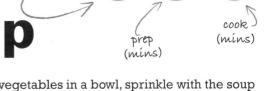

serves **1** 2 0
prep (mins)   cook (mins)

You can make this even if you only have a kettle. It's a cheat, of course, but actually tastes really good. Plus adding the canned vegetables does add some nutritional value to the mix.

1 Put the vegetables in a bowl, sprinkle with the soup powder, then gradually stir in the boiling water until thoroughly blended.

2 Leave to stand for 1 minute, then stir, sprinkle with the Parmesan, and enjoy.

225 g/1 small can diced mixed vegetables, drained
1 sachet instant golden vegetable soup
1 mug boiling water
1 tsp grated Parmesan-style cheese

Tomato soup with mozzarella

Another instant option for when time and inclination are in short supply. Mozzarella isn't cheap, but you need to buy it fresh so you often find it marked down when near its sell-by date. Buy it then and use it in the next day or so.

1 Mix the cheese, tomato and basil in a bowl, then sprinkle with the soup powder.

2 Pour over the boiling water, stirring all the time, and keep stirring until everything is well blended and the cheese has melted.

½ small round Mozzarella cheese, finely diced
1 tomato, finely chopped
Pinch of dried basil
1 sachet instant tomato soup
1 mug boiling water

Fish finger & mayonnaise

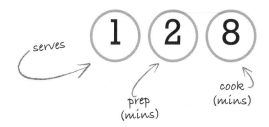

serves · 1 · 2 · 8

prep (mins)

cook (mins)

You can use breaded fish instead of the fingers, but it'll probably work out more expensive and will take a little longer to cook. Beware of economy fish fingers, they're made of minced dubious bits of fish – go for a fish fillet brand.

1 Cook the fish fingers according to the packet directions.

2 Split the roll in half and lay the fish fingers on the bottom half.

3 Top with a slice of cheese and flash under a hot grill to melt the cheese.

4 Top with some tartare sauce or mayonnaise, shredded lettuce and then the lid of the roll.

4 fish fingers
1 soft bread roll
1 slice of cheese
Ready-made tartare sauce or mayonnaise
Lettuce, shredded

Nachos

serves

1-2   5   3

prep
(mins)

cook
(mins)

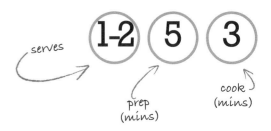

The rest of the salsa will keep in the fridge. Look out for economy corn tortilla chips in supermarkets – they're fine for this, though some may be broken. Use all but the smallest pieces, then crush the bits and sprinkle on top.

1 small bag plain corn tortilla chips
1 jar mild tomato salsa dip
Large handful of grated Cheddar cheese

1   Preheat the grill. Arrange the chips in a shallow flameproof dish or casserole dish.

2   Put a teaspoon of salsa on each one.

3   Cover with grated cheese and grill until the cheese has melted. Serve straight away and enjoy!

Spicy potato cakes

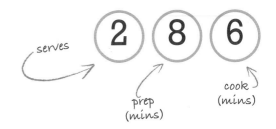

serves **2**

prep (mins) **8**

cook (mins) **6**

These make a tasty lunch or supper dish on their own or topped with fried eggs. You can use curry powder instead of the garam masala and chilli powder if that's what's in the cupboard – or just make them plain without the spices.

2 large <u>potatoes</u>, grated (no need to peel)
1 small <u>onion</u>, grated
½ tsp <u>garam masala</u>
¼ tsp <u>chilli powder</u>
1 <u>egg</u>, beaten
1 tsp <u>plain flour</u>
<u>Salt and pepper</u>
A little <u>oil</u>
SERVE WITH
<u>Mango chutney</u> or other <u>pickle</u>
and <u>salad</u>

1 Mix together the potatoes, onion, spices, egg and flour to combine.

2 Heat enough oil just to cover base of a frying pan, then add spoonfuls of the mixture to make little cakes, pressing down well. Fry for 2–3 minutes until golden brown underneath.

3 Turn them over and fry for a further 2–3 minutes until the other side is browned and the cakes are cooked through.

4 Serve hot with mango chutney or other pickle and salad.

Bacon butty

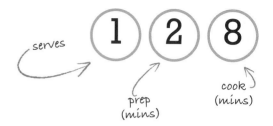

serves 1   2   8

prep (mins)

cook (mins)

I didn't think anyone would need a recipe for this basic essential but my student daughter assures me there are some who do. Fry an egg (see page 15) and add it to the sandwich for a good hangover remedy.

2 back bacon rashers, rinds removed
2 slices of bread
Butter or margarine
Tomato ketchup or brown sauce (optional)

1 Grill the bacon for about 4 minutes on each side until lightly browned and cooked how you like it.

2 Alternatively, lay the rashers on a plate, cover with another plate or greaseproof paper and microwave on High for 45 seconds to 2 minutes until cooked how you like it.

3 Meanwhile, spread the bread with a little butter or margarine. Spread one slice with ketchup or brown sauce, if liked.

4 Lift the bacon on to one slice and top with the other one.

Pitta pockets

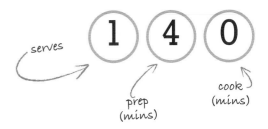

serves **1**

prep (mins) **4**

cook (mins) **0**

It's worth bothering to warm the breads first – as in step 1. If they are cold, they'll often split, stick together, crumble or tear, which is really annoying if you want to fill them, and it's very messy when you come to eat them.

1 Toast or microwave the pittas just to heat through enough to puff up. Split along one long edge to form a pocket.

2 Add the shredded lettuce, tomato, cucumber and one of the suggested fillings.

3 Finish with the mayonnaise.

2 pitta breads
Handful of lettuce, shredded
1 tomato, sliced
A few slices of cucumber
FOR THE FILLING CHOOSE FROM
Tuna, chopped ham, mashed pilchards, sliced corned beef, chopped frankfurter, salami, hard-boiled egg
1 tbsp mayonnaise

Quesadillas

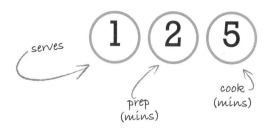

serves

1 2 5

prep (mins)

cook (mins)

Get adventurous and add other fillings – like ham, chorizo or just a spoonful of tomato salsa – anything you like. Just spread it evenly and not too thickly. Keep the rest of the tortillas wrapped in the fridge or freeze for another day.

2 flour tortillas

Handful of grated Cheddar cheese

SERVE WITH

Salad – whatever you like

1 Heat a non-stick frying pan big enough to take the flour tortilla flat. When it feels hot when you hold your hand about 5 cm/2 in above the surface, turn the heat to moderate and add one of the tortillas.

2 Quickly spread the cheese over and top with the second tortilla. Press it down firmly with a fish slice. Fry for a couple of minutes until the cheese is melting and the base is browning slightly, pressing down all the time.

3 Carefully flip the whole thing over, using your hand to guide it (or invert it on to a plate and slide back in). Fry the other side until the cheese has completely melted. Slide on to a plate and cut in wedges.

4 Serve with salad bits.

Stuffed naan bread **wedges**

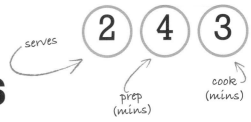

serves **2** **4** **3**

prep (mins) cook (mins)

Pease pudding is really cheap – it's basically just cooked dried split peas. You can mash other canned pulses, like red kidney beans, instead and try mixing them with chilli relish instead of the curry paste and chutney.

2 naan breads
225 g/1 small can pease pudding
2 tsp curry paste
2 tbsp mango chutney
Lemon juice (optional)
Shredded lettuce or other sliced salad stuffs (optional)

1 Grill or microwave the naan bread according to the packet directions.

2 Heat the pease pudding with the curry paste in a saucepan for about 4 minutes until hot, stirring continuously.

3 Spread the pease pudding mixture over the surface of the naan bread.

4 Spread with mango chutney and sprinkle with lemon juice, if using. Add the shredded lettuce, if liked.

5 Fold in half, then cut into manageable wedges.

6 Wrap in kitchen paper and eat in your fingers.

Cheese & salami **croissant**

serves ① ② ③
prep (mins)
cook (mins)

As an alternative, you can spread the croissant with soft garlic and herb cheese and add some chopped red pepper before grilling. Or you can use a slice of ham instead of the salami, or chorizo, grilled bacon or what you fancy.

1 Split the croissant almost in half and fill with the folded salami and cheese slices.

2 Place under a moderate grill for a few minutes until the cheese melts, turning once. Take care not to let it burn.

1 croissant
2 slices of salami
1 slice of cheese
SERVE WITH
Tomato wedges

Hot chilli dogs

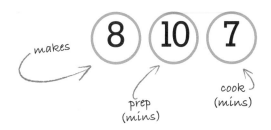

makes **8** **10** **7**

prep (mins)   cook (mins)

If you aren't sharing these with friends, make up as many as you can eat, then store the remaining chilli mix and hot dogs in plastic containers with lids or in sealed plastic bags in the fridge and heat and eat over the next couple of days.

Large knob of <u>butter</u> or <u>margarine</u>
1 <u>onion</u>, thinly sliced
1 <u>green pepper</u>, thinly sliced
¼ tsp <u>chilli powder</u>
<u>Tomato ketchup</u>
425 g/1 large can <u>hot dog</u> <u>sausages</u>
8 <u>finger rolls</u>

1 Melt the butter or margarine in a small saucepan. Add the onion and pepper and fry for 2 minutes, stirring constantly.

2 Stir in the chilli powder. Cover and cook gently for 5 minutes or until the onion and pepper are tender. Moisten to taste with a little tomato ketchup.

3 Meanwhile, heat the hot dogs according to the instructions on the can.

4 Split the rolls and spread them with the chilli mixture. Add a hot dog to each and serve at once.

Tuna & chilli mayo wraps

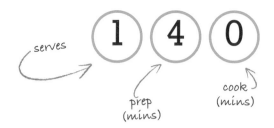

serves **1**

prep (mins) **4**

cook (mins) **0**

Try this with chopped seafood sticks or thawed frozen prawns (if you can get some on special offer). Add different salad stuffs, too, like sliced tomatoes, spinach leaves instead of lettuce or some sliced radishes.

1 tbsp <u>mayonnaise</u>

1 tbsp <u>chilli relish</u> or <u>sweet chilli dipping sauce</u>

100 g/½ small can <u>tuna</u>, well drained

A few torn <u>lettuce leaves</u>

1 <u>flour tortilla</u>

A few slices of <u>cucumber</u>

1　Mix the mayonnaise with the chilli relish or sauce.

2　Stir in the drained tuna.

3　Lay a few torn lettuce leaves on the tortilla. Spread on the tuna mixture, then top with cucumber slices. Fold the bottom and sides of the tortilla up over the filling, then fold in half to form a filled pocket. Alternatively, fold the bottom third up over the filling then roll up from the sides.

TIP: Use the rest of the tuna, mixed with mayo to top a jacket potato, or shred into cooked rice for another meal.

Mushroom
omelette **baguette**

serves **1**

prep (mins) **5**

cook (mins) **5**

Eggs have had a bad press in recent years but they are a good, nutritious food – as well as being quick and easy to cook. Buy eggs with the Lion mark, keep them in the fridge and watch the use-by date.

1 small <u>French stick</u>
<u>Butter</u> or <u>margarine</u>
2 <u>eggs</u>
2 tbsp <u>water</u>
¼ tsp <u>dried mixed herbs</u>
<u>Salt and pepper</u>
2-3 <u>mushrooms</u>, sliced

1 Warm the French stick either in the oven or under the grill, turning frequently. Cut a slit along the length and spread with butter or margarine.

2 Meanwhile, break the eggs in a bowl. Add the water, herbs and some salt and pepper. Beat well with a whisk or fork.

3 Heat a frying pan and add a knob of butter or margarine. When sizzling, add the mushrooms and fry, stirring for 2 minutes. Pour in the egg mixture. Lift and stir the mixture with a fish slice or spatula for a few minutes until set.

4 Slide the omelette out on to a plate and roll up. Lay it in the French stick and cut in half.

Croque monsieur

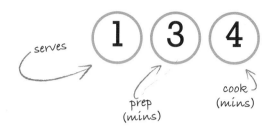

serves **1**

prep (mins) **3**

cook (mins) **4**

This is the classic French toasted ham and cheese sandwich. You can top Monsieur with a fried or poached egg to turn it into a Croque Madame. It works with any kind of ham, chorizo, pepperoni or what you will.

2 slices of <u>bread</u>
<u>Butter</u> or <u>margarine</u>
1 slice of <u>ham</u>
1 slice of <u>cheese</u> or a small handful of grated <u>Cheddar</u> <u>cheese</u>

1. Spread the bread with butter or margarine. Keeping buttered sides out, sandwich together with the ham and cheese.

2. Either grill under a hot grill for about 2 minutes on each side until golden and the cheese has melted, or heat a frying pan and fry, pressing down with a fish slice and turning once. Cut in halves and serve immediately.

Cheese & onion sandwich

serves **1**

prep **3** (mins)

cook **4** (mins)

There are any number of variations on a hot sandwich, so use your imagination – and whatever is in the cupboard. Of course, if you have a sandwich toaster, you can use that to toast your sandwich instead.

2 slices of bread
Butter or margarine
1 slice of cheese or a small handful of grated Cheddar cheese
1 small onion, sliced and separated into rings
Pinch of dried mixed herbs

1 Spread the bread with butter or margarine. Keeping buttered sides out, sandwich together with the cheese, onion rings and herbs.

2 Either grill under a hot grill for about 2 minutes on each side until golden and the cheese has melted, or heat a frying pan and fry, pressing down with a fish slice and turning once. Cut in halves and serve immediately.

Swiss cheese & pineapple

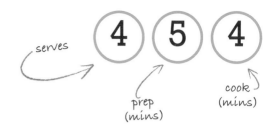

serves **4**
prep (mins) **5**
cook (mins) **4**

A whole can of pineapple rings will make four toasts. If you only want two, use half and chop the rest to eat for dessert or sprinkled on your cereal. Buy fruit in juice rather than syrup – it tastes better and you don't need the extra sugar.

4 slices of <u>wholemeal bread</u>
<u>Butter</u> or <u>margarine</u>
2 tbsp <u>tomato purée</u>
4 slices of <u>ham</u>
225 g/1 small can <u>pineapple slices</u>, drained
4 slices of <u>Gruyère</u> or <u>Emmental cheese</u>
1 <u>tomato</u>, cut into 4 slices
½ tsp <u>dried basil</u>

1 Preheat the grill and toast the bread on one side only. Butter the untoasted sides and place on the grill rack.

2 Spread with the tomato purée, then top with the slices of ham, pineapple and cheese.

3 Put a slice of tomato on top of each and sprinkle with basil. Grill for a few minutes until the cheese melts and bubbles. Serve hot.

Omelette with green beans

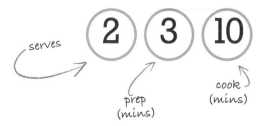

serves **2** **3** **10**

prep (mins)

cook (mins)

If you're feeling decadent, canned asparagus spears taste great served like this or, for a more Asian flavour, add drained, canned or fresh bean sprouts instead and sprinkle with soy sauce before rolling up.

4 eggs
4 tbsp cold water
Salt and pepper
1 tsp dried mixed herbs
Butter or margarine
300 g/1 medium can whole green beans, drained
SERVE WITH
Crusty bread and chunky salad pieces

1 Beat one of the eggs in a bowl with 1 tbsp of water, a little salt and pepper and ¼ tsp herbs.

2 Heat a little butter or margarine in a frying pan. Pour in the egg and fry, lifting the edge and letting uncooked egg run underneath until set. Transfer to a plate and leave to cool while you make 3 more omelettes in the same way.

3 Divide the beans between the omelettes and roll them up.

4 Serve with crusty bread and chunky salad pieces that can be eaten with your fingers.

Creamy tuna dip

Try this dip as a sandwich filler, spread on tortillas with some shredded lettuce or sliced cucumber for wraps, or spooned on jacket potatoes. Or simply grab some tortilla chips or carrot sticks and dip in.

1 Put the tuna in a bowl and break up with a wooden spoon. Beat in the remaining ingredients until well blended.

2 Serve with vegetable dippers such as small florets of cauliflower, sticks of cucumber, carrot and green or red pepper and fingers of crisp toast or chunks of French bread.

200 g/1 small can tuna, drained

4 tbsp mayonnaise

3 tbsp plain yoghurt

1 tbsp tomato ketchup

1 tsp vinegar or lemon juice

Salt and pepper

SERVE WITH

Sticks of carrot, cucumber, courgette or other vegetable dippers, tortilla chips, fingers of toast or chunks of French bread

Tuna & cream cheese pâté

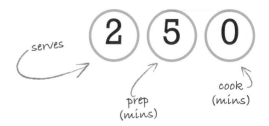

serves **2**

prep (mins) **5**

cook (mins) **0**

If you want to make this look flash, arrange some lettuce leaves on plates, pile this on top with a sprinkling of black pepper and serve with tomato wedges alongside. It will keep in a covered container in the fridge for several days.

1 Mash the tuna in a bowl with the cheese.

2 Add the remaining ingredients and mix well.

3 Chill, if you have time, until ready to serve.

4 Serve with hot toast and tomato wedges.

200 g/1 small can <u>tuna</u>, drained

200 g/1 small carton <u>white soft cheese</u>

Splash of <u>vinegar</u> or <u>lemon juice</u>

Pinch of <u>chilli powder</u>

<u>Salt and pepper</u>

½ <u>cucumber</u>, diced

SERVE WITH

<u>Hot toast</u> and <u>tomato wedges</u>

French toast

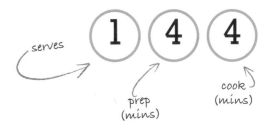

serves 1

prep (mins) 4

cook (mins) 4

This is plain old 'eggy bread' – a great breakfast dish or good for a snack any time. An alternative is a fried egg sandwich: two slices of buttered bread, smeared with tomato ketchup or brown sauce and filled with two fried eggs.

1 Beat the eggs with the milk and a little salt and pepper in a shallow dish.

2 Cut each slice of bread into 4 triangles and dip into the egg mixture. Leave to soak in completely.

3 Heat enough oil to cover the base of the frying pan. Fry the soaked bread for a few minutes until golden brown on both sides. Sprinkle with salt and pepper and serve hot.

2 eggs
1 tbsp milk
Salt and pepper
3 slices of bread
Oil for frying

Cheese & onion pitta

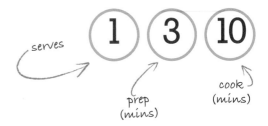

serves **1**

prep (mins) **3**

cook (mins) **10**

Olive oil gives this a lovely flavour but don't buy it specially. Try adding a few sliced olives to the mixture or, for extra flavour, smear the pitta with a little pesto from a jar before adding the fried onions.

1 tbsp oil
1 onion, sliced
1/2 tsp garlic from a jar or tube
1 pitta bread
2–3 slices of Cheddar or Mozzarella cheese
SERVE WITH
Sliced tomatoes

1 Heat half the oil in a frying pan. Add the onion and garlic and cook over a moderate heat, stirring, for 3–4 minutes until the sliced onion is soft and lightly golden.

2 Spoon on to the pitta bread and spread out evenly.

3 Put the pan back over a low heat and add the remaining oil. Add the pitta bread, onion-side up, and top with the cheese. Cover the pan with a lid, plate or foil and cook gently for about 4 minutes until the cheese has completely melted.

4 Serve hot with some sliced tomatoes.

Spiced
mushrooms

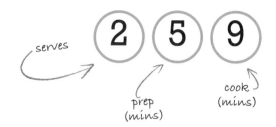

serves **2**

prep (mins) **5**

cook (mins) **9**

Turn this into a substantial main meal by adding a drained 425 g/large can of chick peas at step 3. Serve with lots of crusty bread and a green salad instead of on toast. Delicious and very filling.

1 tbsp <u>oil</u>
1 small <u>onion</u>, finely chopped
8 <u>mushrooms</u>, quartered
2 <u>tomatoes</u>, chopped
2 tsp <u>tomato ketchup</u>
2 tsp <u>Worcestershire sauce</u>
Pinch of <u>chilli powder</u>
SERVE WITH
<u>Hot buttered toast</u>

1 Heat the oil in a saucepan and fry the onion for 2 minutes, stirring, until softened.

2 Add the mushrooms and tomatoes and cook, stirring, for 2 minutes.

3 Add the remaining ingredients and simmer, stirring, for about 5 minutes or until the mushrooms are just cooked but most of the liquid has evaporated, stirring occasionally.

4 Serve on hot buttered toast.

Herb & salami garlic bread

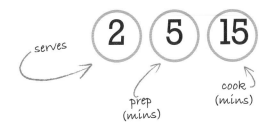

serves **2**
prep (mins) **5**
cook (mins) **15**

It's hardly worth making your own garlic baguettes as they are so cheap, but customising them is fun. For this one, you could use sliced ham instead of salami, or just sliced tomatoes and cheese tucked between each slice.

1 ready-to-bake garlic baguette
8–12 slices of salami
1 tsp dried mixed herbs or oregano
Salt and pepper

1. Preheat the oven to 200°C/400°F/gas 6/fan oven 180°C.

2. Unwrap the garlic bread and ease the slices open gently. Tuck a slice of salami in between each slice. Sprinkle with the herbs.

3. Wrap in foil, shiny-side in, and bake in the oven for about 15 minutes until the crust feels crisp but the centre is still soft.

Hot pastrami on **rye**

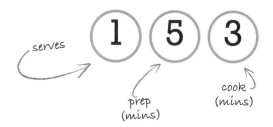

serves **1** 5 3

prep (mins)

cook (mins)

At its home in New York, it is often served with a pimento-based thousand island dressing, but I prefer the mustard and chilli soft cheese. You can use wholemeal or any other bread. It's also good with corned beef or streaky bacon.

2 slices of <u>dark rye bread</u>
1 tbsp white <u>soft cheese</u>
½ tsp <u>Dijon mustard</u>
Pinch of <u>chilli powder</u> or a few drops of <u>Tabasco sauce</u>
4 thin slices of <u>pastrami</u>
<u>Sunflower oil</u>
<u>Pepper</u>
2 <u>gherkins</u> (cornichons), halved lengthways (optional)
SERVE WITH
<u>Coleslaw</u>

1 Preheat the grill, then toast the bread slices on one side.

2 Mash the cheese and mustard together with the chilli powder or Tabasco and spread over the untoasted sides. Place on a plate.

3 Place the pastrami on foil on the grill rack. Brush or smear with oil and grill until just beginning to sizzle.

4 Place on top of the cheese, sprinkle with pepper and top each with a halved gherkin, if using.

5 Serve straight away with coleslaw.

Smoked
mackerel **bagels**

serves **1**

prep (mins) **5**

cook (mins) **0**

Smoked mackerel fillets often come in vacuum packs of two. Wrap the other thoroughly in foil and store in the fridge or freeze and use within two months. You could use it for one-pot kedgeree on page 158.

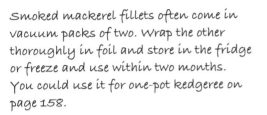

1 smoked mackerel fillet
1-2 bagels, split in half
2 tbsp white soft cheese
2 tsp horseradish relish
A little lemon juice
Pepper
Salad cress, to garnish

1 Cut the smoked mackerel fillet into small pieces, discarding the skin if you don't like it.

2 Spread the halved bagels with the soft cheese. Top with a spreading of horseradish relish, then the mackerel fillet.

3 Sprinkle with lemon juice and add a good grinding of pepper. Top with salad cress and serve.

Easy fish pâté

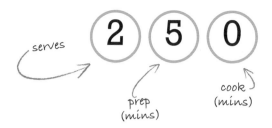

serves **2**
prep (mins) **5**
cook (mins) **0**

Try this spread on bread with a few onion rings on top, or it's good with rye crispbread. If you don't eat it all, it'll keep in the fridge, covered, for 3 days.

1 Put all the ingredients in a bowl.

2 Mix well and blend until smooth.

3 Serve with bread, toast or crispbread.

120 g/small can <u>sardines in oil</u>, drained
Large knob of <u>butter</u> or <u>margarine</u>
2 tbsp <u>plain yoghurt</u>
½ tsp <u>lemon juice</u>
A few drops of <u>Tabasco sauce</u> or a pinch of <u>chilli powder</u>
<u>Salt and pepper</u>
TO SERVE
<u>Bread, toast</u> or <u>crispbread</u>

Cheese & pineapple salad

serves **2** prep (mins) **3** cook (mins) **0**

This is a good way to use up any pineapple left over from another recipe. Or, if you are left with pineapple from this, eat it for dessert or on your cereal. It also goes well with bacon.

1. Mix together the pineapple, cheese, walnuts, chives and pepper.

2. Put some lettuce in a bowl and top with the salad. Sprinkle with paprika, if liked.

3. Serve with crackers or bread.

1 canned pineapple ring, chopped
1 small carton cottage cheese
1 tbsp chopped walnuts
1 tsp dried chives
Pepper
A few lettuce leaves
Paprika (optional)
TO SERVE
Crackers or bread

Chicken & pesto **baguette**

 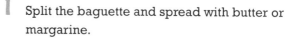
Pesto is a useful thing to have in the fridge. You can stir it into hot pasta, spice up leftover rice to serve cold, or use it with leftover chicken or sliced chicken or ham to make a tasty sandwich.

1 Split the baguette and spread with butter or margarine.

2 Line with the lettuce.

3 Mix the pesto, mayonnaise and chicken and pile into the baguette. Sprinkle with pine nuts, if using.

1 sandwich baguette or roll
Butter or margarine
1 lettuce leaf
1 tbsp pesto
1 tbsp mayonnaise
2 slices cooked chicken, chopped
A few pine nuts (optional)

Tzatziki with pittas

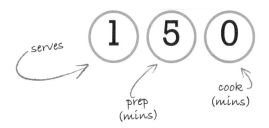

serves 1
prep (mins) 5
cook (mins) 0

You can make your own version of this classic Greek dip in minutes – and it is cheaper than buying it ready made. Use anything you have to dip in – pittas, toast, sticks of vegetables, crackers or crisps. Thick yoghurt works best.

1 Squeeze the grated cucumber to remove all the excess moisture.

2 Mix together everything except the pittas. If you have time, leave in the fridge for a few hours.

3 Cut the pittas into strips and serve with the dip.

5 cm piece of cucumber, grated
5 tbsp Greek-style plain yoghurt
1 tsp olive oil
½ tsp garlic purée
1 tsp dried mint
Salt and pepper
Pitta breads

Vegetarian
meals

This is a big section because the recipes are great whether or not you are veggie – and going meat-free some days, at least, can really save you money.

If you are cooking for vegans or strict vegetarians, remember that many don't eat dairy products so watch out for milk and eggs, and make sure any cheese you use is suitable (read the labels) – real Parmesan, for example, is not vegetarian. Ready-made sauces – such as Worcestershire sauce – also often contain animal products, so keep an eye on them as well.

I haven't used tofu or Quorn because they are expensive but you can use minced Quorn instead of mince or tofu instead of fish.

ntil & vegetable soup

serves · 2 · prep (mins) 10 · cook (mins) 20

Dried red lentils are cheap to buy, packed with protein and cook without soaking first. You can keep the rest of the swede in the chiller box of the fridge for up to a week or two.

¼ mug red lentils

2 mugs water

1 onion, chopped

1 potato, cut in small dice

1 carrot, cut in small dice

¼ small swede, cut in small dice

1 vegetable stock cube

1 tbsp tomato purée

Large pinch of dried mixed herbs

Salt and pepper

SERVE WITH

Crusty bread

1 Put everything in a saucepan. Bring to the boil, stir, reduce the heat until gently bubbling round the edges, part-cover and cook for about 20 minutes until everything is tender.

2 Taste and re-season, if necessary. Either serve as it is, chunky, or mash with a potato masher or purée with a hand blender.

3 Serve with crusty bread.

Cheese & sweetcorn soup

To turn this into a chowder, dice the potatoes instead of slicing. Use 2 mugs of water and the stock cubes to cook the veggies. Stir in a couple of mugs of milk at step 4 and don't mash the potatoes before stirring in the cheese.

Knob of butter or margarine
1 onion, chopped
4 potatoes, sliced
300 g/1 medium can sweetcorn
4 mugs boiling water
2 vegetable stock cubes
Salt and pepper
½ mug grated Cheddar cheese
SERVE WITH
Bread or rolled up flour tortillas

1 Melt the butter or margarine in a saucepan and fry the onion over a fairly high heat for 2 minutes, stirring, until the onion softens and is just turning pale golden.

2 Add the remaining ingredients, except the cheese, and heat until boiling.

3 Turn down the heat until bubbling gently around the edges, part-cover the pan and cook for a further 20 minutes.

4 Mash the potatoes into the liquid with a potato masher. Stir in the cheese. Taste and re-season if necessary. Heat, stirring, until the cheese melts.

almost finished

5 Serve with bread or soft tortillas.

Double tomato & **bean soup**

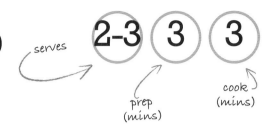

serves **2-3** **3** prep (mins) **3** cook (mins)

Try this with some garlic pittas. Mash 2 knobs of butter or margarine with about ½ tsp garlic from a jar or tube and spread it over a couple of pitta breads. Put on foil on the grill rack and grill until the butter melts. Cut in pieces.

300 g/1 medium can <u>condensed tomato soup</u>

400 g/1 large can <u>chopped tomatoes</u>

425 g/1 large can <u>haricot beans</u>, drained

½ tsp <u>dried basil</u>

SERVE WITH

<u>Garlic bread</u>

1 Empty the can of condensed tomato soup into a saucepan. Add one canful of water, whisking with a metal whisk.

2 Stir in the chopped tomatoes, beans and basil.

3 Heat through, stirring, until almost boiling.

4 Ladle into bowls and serve with garlic bread.

TIP I've used canned beans for quickness and many supermarket own brands and less well-known makes are very cheap; but if you cook a batch of dried beans from scratch you'll save even more money.

Soak the dried beans in cold water for a couple of hours. Put in fresh water and boil rapidly for 10 minutes, to destroy any toxins, then reduce the heat and simmer so they are gently bubbling for 45 minutes to 1 hour, depending on the type, until they are tender. Don't add salt or you'll toughen them. Top up with more boiling water during cooking if necessary. Once cooked, drain and store in a covered container in the fridge for several days to use as required, or pack in plastic bags in usable amounts. (A 450 g pack of dried beans is the equivalent of 4 x 425g/large cans.)

Brown onion soup

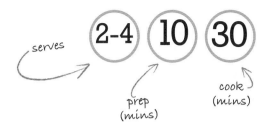

serves 2-4   prep (mins) 10   cook (mins) 30

This is a simple version of the classic French onion soup. It's worth taking the time to cook the onions a while to get them rich and brown. You can cheat and use a can of fried onions, but drain off any excess oil, and continue from step 2.

Large knob of <u>butter</u> or <u>margarine</u>
4 large <u>onions</u>, roughly chopped
2 tsp <u>sugar</u>
4 mugs <u>water</u>
2 <u>vegetable stock cubes</u>
<u>Salt and pepper</u>
2–4 slices of <u>French bread</u> (or ½–1 slice from a large square loaf)
A little grated <u>Cheddar cheese</u>

1 Melt the butter or margarine in a saucepan and fry the onions for 5 minutes, stirring until soft and turning brown.

2 Add the sugar and continue frying for 3–4 minutes until a rich golden brown, stirring all the time.

3 Stir in the water, stock cubes and a little salt and pepper, bring to the boil, reduce the heat, part-cover and simmer, bubbling gently, for 15–20 minutes until the onions are really soft. Taste and re-season.

4 Meanwhile toast the bread. If using a slice from a loaf, cut it in half or quarters after toasting, to make small squares. Cover with the cheese and grill until melting.

5 Spoon the soup into bowls and top with the toasted cheese.

Curried
vegetable **soup**

If you like coconut, it's cheaper to buy a box of powder and reconstitute it instead of buying the cans. You can freeze any remaining coriander, then just crumble it in dishes from frozen.

¼ tsp garlic from a jar or tube

1–2 tsp curry paste

1 tbsp oil

¼ x 1 kg pack frozen mixed vegetables

1 mug boiling water

1 vegetable stock cube

400 g/1 large can coconut milk

1 tbsp tomato purée

Salt and pepper

Small handful of fresh coriander, chopped

SERVE WITH

Garlic and coriander naan breads

1 Fry the garlic and curry paste in the oil for a few seconds.

2 Add the vegetables, stock, coconut milk and tomato purée, bring to the boil, reduce the heat, part-cover and simmer so it bubbles gently for 15 minutes until the vegetables are tender.

3 Season to taste and stir in the coriander. Ladle into warm bowls.

4 Serve with garlic and coriander naan breads.

Minestrone

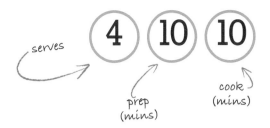

serves 4 — prep 10 (mins) — cook 10 (mins)

This is really filling and it's worth making a potful to eat over a few days. You can crumble in a bit of spaghetti instead of the macaroni, add grated courgette or swede instead of the parsnip or throw in sweetcorn instead of peas.

1 tbsp oil
1 small onion, chopped
1 carrot, grated
1 small parsnip, grated
¼ small cabbage, shredded
½ mug frozen peas
Small handful of quick-cook macaroni
400 g/1 large can tomatoes
425 g/1 large can haricot beans
2 mugs water
1 vegetable stock cube
½ tsp dried oregano or mixed herbs
Salt and pepper
SERVE WITH
Grated Parmesan-style or Cheddar cheese and crusty bread

1 Heat the oil in a large pan and fry the onion for 1 minute, stirring.

2 Add the remaining ingredients, including the liquid in the can of beans, breaking up the tomatoes with a wooden spoon.

3 Bring to the boil, reduce the heat and simmer, bubbling gently, for 10 minutes, or until the vegetables and pasta are soft. Taste and re-season if necessary.

4 Serve in soup bowls with cheese to sprinkle over and crusty bread.

Peanut soup

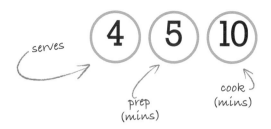

prep (mins)

cook (mins)

This recipe is so easy, you might as well make enough for two days. If you like spice, add a pinch of chilli powder with the flour or spike it at the end with a few drops of Tabasco to taste. For crunch, sprinkle with a few chopped peanuts.

Large knob of <u>butter</u> or <u>margarine</u>
1 small <u>onion</u>, grated
1 <u>carrot</u>, grated
3 tbsp <u>plain flour</u>
4 mugs <u>boiling water</u>
2 <u>vegetable stock cubes</u>
½ jar <u>smooth peanut butter</u>
1 mug <u>single cream</u> or <u>milk</u>
SERVE WITH
<u>Crusty bread</u>

1   Melt the butter or margarine in a large pan and fry the onion and carrot for 2 minutes, stirring.

2   Sprinkle in the flour and cook, stirring, for 1 minute. Remove from the heat.

3   Gradually blend in the boiling water, stirring all the time, and add the stock cubes. Return to the heat, bring to the boil, stirring, turn down the heat and cook gently for 5 minutes.

4   Blend in the peanut butter and cream or milk, using a whisk or wooden spoon. Reheat, stirring all the time, but do not boil.

5   Serve in warm soup bowls or mugs with lots of crusty bread.

66 vegetarian meals

Macaroni
cheese

If you only have one pan, you'll have to cook the macaroni first and then make the sauce. You can serve it on its own or with some grilled bacon. I like it with some grilled tomatoes served on the side.

4 large handfuls of short-cut macaroni
3 tbsp plain flour
1 mug milk
Large knob of butter or margarine
1 tsp mustard (optional)
2 large handfuls of Cheddar cheese, grated
Salt and pepper
1 Weetabix or a handful of bran flakes and a little extra grated cheese (optional)

1 Cook the macaroni according to the packet directions. Drain and return to the saucepan.

2 Meanwhile, whisk the flour with a little of the milk in a separate saucepan until smooth. Whisk in the remaining milk and add the butter or margarine. Bring to the boil and boil for 2 minutes, whisking all the time, until thick and smooth.

3 Stir in the mustard and cheese and season to taste with salt and pepper. Add to the pasta and stir well to combine.

4 Either serve straight away or spoon into a flameproof dish, top with the crumbled Weetabix or crushed bran flakes and sprinkle with a little extra grated cheese. Grill until golden brown and bubbling.

Chilli vegetables with **baked eggs**

serves **2** prep (mins) **10** cook (mins) **25**

If you prefer no fire, give the dish a Mediterranean feel: omit the chilli and add a pinch of dried basil instead. If eating alone, spoon out half the mixture before adding just 2 eggs, then heat the rest and cook more eggs the next day.

2 tbsp olive or sunflower oil
1 onion, chopped
1 small aubergine, diced
1 green pepper, diced
1 red chilli, seeds removed and chopped (or ¼ tsp chilli powder)
425 g/1 large can black eyed beans, drained
½ mug boiling water
½ vegetable stock cube
2 tbsp tomato purée or ketchup
Salt and pepper
4 eggs
SERVE WITH
Corn tortilla chips and a salad

1 Heat the oil in a large frying pan. Add the vegetables and chilli and fry for 5 minutes, stirring until softened.

2 Add the beans, water, stock cube, tomato purée or ketchup. Season lightly. Stir well, turn down the heat, cover and simmer very gently for about 10 minutes until really soft, stirring once or twice.

3 Make 4 'wells' in the mixture. Break an egg into each. Cover again and cook gently for 5–10 minutes until cooked to your liking.

4 Serve straight from the pan with corn tortilla chips and a salad.

Vegetable
cottage pie

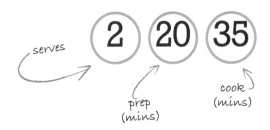

serves **2** prep (mins) **20** cook (mins) **35**

This takes a bit more time to prepare but it isn't difficult and tastes good. It's ideal when you're eating with a friend but, if not, leftovers can be reheated until piping hot and served the next day.

2–3 large potatoes, cut into smallish chunks
Knob of butter or margarine
1 tbsp milk
1/4 x 1 kg packet of frozen chunky mixed vegetables
1 slice of wholemeal bread, chopped
400 g/1 large can baked beans
1 tsp Marmite, or other yeast extract
2 tbsp boiling water
1/2 tsp dried mixed herbs
Salt and pepper
Large handful of grated Cheddar cheese

1 Boil the potatoes in lightly salted water for about 4 minutes until just tender. Drain and mash with a potato masher or fork. Beat in the butter or margarine and the milk.

2 Preheat the oven to 200°C/400°F/gas 6/fan oven 180°C.

3 Meanwhile, bring a pan of lightly salted water to the boil, add the vegetables and boil for about 3 minutes until just tender. Drain.

4 Mix the vegetables with the bread and beans in an ovenproof serving dish.

5 Blend the yeast extract with the water. Stir into the dish with the herbs until thoroughly mixed. Season to taste.

6 Top with the mashed potato, then sprinkle with the cheese. Bake in the oven for about 35 minutes until golden.

Swiss cheese & potato bake

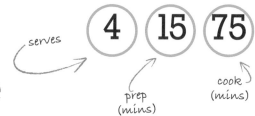

serves **4** — prep (mins) **15** — cook (mins) **75**

It's worth making enough for four people – if you don't eat it all at once, the rest will keep in the fridge and is delicious eaten cold with pickles. You can, of course, use Cheddar or Edam – or any hard cheese – instead of Swiss cheese.

3–4 large <u>potatoes</u>, thinly sliced
Knob of <u>butter</u> or <u>margarine</u>
1½ mugs grated <u>Gruyère</u> or <u>Emmental cheese</u>
<u>Salt and pepper</u>
2 <u>eggs</u>
150 ml/1 small carton <u>single cream</u>
½ mug <u>milk</u>
1 tsp <u>garlic</u> from a jar or tube
SERVE WITH
<u>Salad</u>

1 Put the sliced potatoes in a saucepan of cold water. Bring to the boil and cook for 2 minutes. Drain in a colander, then rinse with cold water to cool them quickly.

2 Preheat the oven to 180°C/350°F/gas 4/fan oven 160°C. Use the butter or margarine to grease an ovenproof serving dish big enough to take about 5 mugfuls of water.

3 Put a layer of potato slices in the base. Cover with a little of the cheese and a little salt and pepper. Repeat the layers until all the potatoes and cheese are used, finishing with a layer of cheese.

4 Whisk the eggs, cream and milk together with the garlic in a small bowl, then pour over the potatoes.

5 Bake in the oven for about 1–1¼ hours until the potatoes are tender and the top is golden brown.

almost finished

6 Serve hot with salad.

Spaghetti with tomato **sauce**

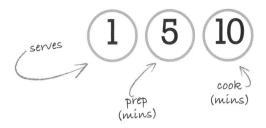

serves 1 · prep 5 (mins) · cook 10 (mins)

It's worth having a pot of fresh basil on the windowsill as it tastes great thrown into all sorts of dishes at the last minute, from pizzas to salads. You can use a pinch of dried basil instead but it's not quite the same.

1 tbsp olive or sunflower oil
1 small onion, chopped
2 large ripe tomatoes, chopped
2 tsp tomato purée
Large pinch of sugar, salt and pepper
3 fresh basil leaves, chopped
¼ x 500 g packet of spaghetti
Grated Parmesan-style cheese
SERVE WITH
Green salad

1 Heat the oil in a saucepan and fry the onion, stirring, for 2 minutes.

2 Add the tomatoes, tomato purée and seasoning, turn down the heat as low as possible, cover and cook for 5–10 minutes until pulpy, stirring occasionally. Stir in the basil.

3 Meanwhile cook the spaghetti in boiling water with a pinch of salt, according to the packet directions, until just tender (see page 18). Drain in a colander and return to the pan.

4 Add the tomato sauce and lift and stir to coat each strand in the sauce.

5 Tip into a bowl and sprinkle with grated Parmesan. Serve with a green salad.

Savoury
egg rice

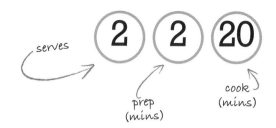

This is fast and cheap. Eat it with a salad to get your five-a-day topped up or, if you're not mad about salad, add a mugful of frozen peas and sweetcorn or diced mixed vegetables to the rice in the frying pan half way through.

1 packet of <u>savoury rice</u> (any flavour)

4 <u>eggs</u>

SERVE WITH

<u>Crusty bread</u> and a large <u>mixed salad</u>

1 Empty the packet of rice into a large frying pan. Add water as directed on the packet and bring to the boil. Cover with a lid and simmer for 15 minutes.

2 Remove the lid and stir. Make 4 'wells' in the rice mixture, break an egg into each, cover and continue cooking over a gentle heat for about 5 minutes or until the eggs are set and cooked to your liking.

3 Serve straight from the pan with bread and salad.

Vegetable
risotto

Risotto rice has a rounded grain and will give you a creamier finish, but it is more expensive. Instead, you can use long-grain, in which case just use 1 mug of stock, add it with the tomatoes, cover and simmer for 20 minutes.

1 onion, chopped
1 carrot, chopped
1 green pepper, chopped
2 tbsp oil
½ mug risotto rice
400 g/1 large can chopped tomatoes
Pinch of dried basil
1½ mugs hot vegetable stock
Salt and pepper
Large handful of grated Cheddar cheese

1 Fry the vegetables in the oil for 5 minutes, stirring.

2 Add the rice and stir until hot and coated in oil.

3 Add the tomatoes and basil and bring to a simmer.

4 Gradually add the hot stock, a bit at a time, stirring and letting it be absorbed before adding more. It will take 15–20 minutes until the rice is cooked.

5 Season and serve sprinkled with the cheese.

Mushroom & nut pilaf

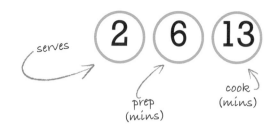

serves **2** prep (mins) **6** cook (mins) **13**

The peanuts add protein and a delicious texture. I prefer to use raw ones but you can use roasted, salted if you prefer (go even easier on the soy sauce though). Cashew nuts taste great in this, but they are more expensive.

½ mug long-grain rice
1 tbsp oil
1 small onion, sliced
1 green pepper, chopped
½ tsp garlic from a jar or tube
8 mushrooms, sliced
Handful of raw peanuts
Soy sauce

1. Cook the rice in plenty of boiling, lightly salted water for 10 minutes until tender, or according to packet directions. Drain.

2. Meanwhile, heat the oil and fry the onion and pepper, stirring for about 5 minutes until softened and lightly golden.

3. Stir in the garlic, mushrooms and peanuts and fry for 1 minute.

4. Add the rice and stir well. Sprinkle with soy sauce to taste, remembering that it is very salty. Fry, stirring, for 2–3 minutes until heated through. Serve at once.

Cheese & mushroom **wedges**

Cottage cheese is an often forgotten ingredient that is low in fat and high in protein. You can use one flavoured with chives or peppers for added flavour, or try adding a grated carrot or courgette instead of the sliced mushrooms.

2 eggs, beaten
200 g/1 small carton cottage cheese
5 tbsp milk
Salt and pepper
4 mushrooms, sliced
1 small onion, chopped
Pinch of dried mixed herbs
Knob of butter or margarine
SERVE WITH
Salad roll or sandwich

1 Mix all the ingredients except the butter or margarine in a bowl. Preheat the grill.

2 Heat a frying pan with the knob of butter or margarine. When sizzling, swirl round to coat the base.

3 Add the omelette mixture and cook over a moderate heat, lifting and stirring until almost set and golden brown underneath.

4 Pop the pan under the grill for a few minutes to brown the top (be careful of the handle).

5 Serve cut into wedges, with a salad roll or sandwich.

Roasted peppers with **Halloumi**

serves **2** **5** **8**

prep (mins)

cook (mins)

Look out for value packs of peppers, or buy a pack of frozen roasted peppers and just heat half a packet through to serve with the Halloumi. You could also use a couple of discs of goats' cheese instead of the Halloumi.

2–3 tbsp olive or sunflower oil
4 peppers, preferably mixed colours, cut in thick slices
1 onion, sliced
Large pinch of dried basil
Salt and pepper
½ block Halloumi cheese, cut in 4 thick slices
SERVE WITH
Crusty bread

1 Heat half the oil in a large frying pan. Add the peppers, onion and basil and fry, stirring, for about 5 minutes until softened but still with a little 'bite'. Season to taste.

2 Put the Halloumi on foil on the grill rack. Smear the remaining oil over both sides. Grill for a few minutes until turning golden in places and softening – no need to turn over.

3 Spoon the peppers on to plates, top with the cheese and serve with lots of crusty bread.

Dhal

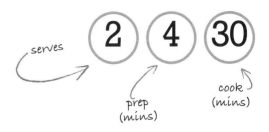

serves 2 4 30
prep (mins)
cook (mins)

Experiment by adding cubes of Cheddar or Edam cheese or paneer (Asian curd cheese) just before serving. For added flavour and authenticity, fry a chopped onion in a little oil until golden and spoon it over the dhal before serving.

1 mug red lentils
1 onion, chopped
1 tsp garlic from a jar or tube
2 tbsp curry powder
2 mugs boiling water
1 vegetable stock cube
Salt and pepper
SERVE WITH
Naan bread or rice with salad
and chutney

1 Put all the ingredients into a saucepan and bring to the boil, stirring occasionally.

2 Reduce the heat and simmer, bubbling gently, for 20–30 minutes until very mushy, stirring frequently to stop it sticking to the bottom of the pan. Add a little more water while cooking if the lentils become too dry. Season to taste.

3 Serve hot with naan bread or rice, salad and chutney.

Mock cheese soufflé

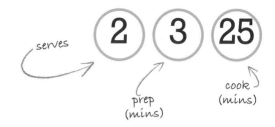

serves **2**
prep (mins) **3**
cook (mins) **25**

This tastes as good as a cheese soufflé but is more substantial and less effort. You can stand the open can of tomatoes on the oven shelf (on foil to catch drips) to heat up while it cooks, or serve it with tomato salad or baked beans.

Large knob of <u>butter</u> or <u>margarine</u>
1 <u>egg</u>, separated (page 20)
½ mug <u>milk</u>
2 thick slices of <u>bread</u>, crusts removed
½ mug grated <u>Cheddar cheese</u>
<u>Salt and pepper</u>
SERVE WITH
<u>Canned tomatoes</u>

1 Preheat the oven to 200°C/400°F/gas 6/fan oven 180°C. Grease an ovenproof dish well with the butter or margarine.

2 Beat the egg yolk with the milk in the greased dish and crumble in the bread. Add the cheese and a little salt and pepper. Leave to stand for 15 minutes.

3 Whisk the egg white until stiff in a clean bowl with a metal balloon whisk and gently fold into the mixture with a metal spoon, using a figure-of-eight motion.

4 Cook in the oven for about 25 minutes until risen and golden.

5 Serve immediately with canned tomatoes.

Bean stew with dumplings

serves 4
prep (mins) 4
cook (mins) 25

This is worth cooking for four and, anyway, is excellent reheated the next day. If you don't fancy the cheese dumplings, simply serve the stew topped with grated cheese and serve with lots of bread or rolls.

400 g/1 large can <u>tomatoes</u>
425 g/1 large can <u>butter beans</u>, drained
425 g/1 large can of <u>black-eyed beans</u>, drained
½ tsp <u>garlic</u> from a jar or tube
1 tbsp <u>tomato purée</u>
200 g/1 small can <u>sweetcorn</u>
300 g/1 medium can cut <u>green beans</u>, undrained
1 mug <u>water</u>
1 <u>vegetable stock cube</u>
½ tsp <u>dried mixed herbs</u>
<u>Salt and pepper</u>
1 packet <u>dumpling mix</u>
½ mug grated <u>Cheddar cheese</u>

1 Empty the tomatoes into a saucepan and break up with a wooden spoon. Add the drained butter beans and black-eyed beans, the garlic, tomato purée, sweetcorn, green beans (with the liquid), water, stock cube, half the herbs and a little salt and pepper. Bring to the boil, reduce the heat, cover and simmer, bubbling gently for 5 minutes.

2 Meanwhile, empty the dumpling mix into a bowl with the cheese and the rest of the herbs. Add enough cold water and mix with a knife to form a soft but not sticky dough. Shape into 8 balls.

3 Arrange the dumplings around the top of the stew, cover and simmer for a further 15–20 minutes until fluffy. Serve hot.

Quick bean bake

A slice of not-too-fresh bread is about the right amount. Crumble it between your fingers and thumb to make rough breadcrumbs, coarsely grate the soft part of the end crust – or instead just crumble Weetabix or crackers.

1 Heat together the ratatouille, red kidney beans, herbs and pepper in a flameproof casserole dish.

2 Mix the breadcrumbs and cheese together and sprinkle over.

3 Grill until the cheese has melted and browned.

425 g/1 large can ratatouille
425 g/1 large can red kidney beans, drained
½ tsp dried mixed herbs
Pepper
½ mug breadcrumbs
½ mug grated Cheddar cheese

Pasta with corn and spinach

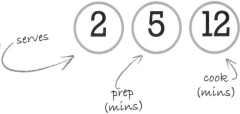

serves **2** prep (mins) **5** cook (mins) **12**

You can make a cheese sauce as for Macaroni cheese (page 67), put the hot pasta mixture in a flameproof dish, cover with the sauce, sprinkle with a little extra cheese and grill until golden and bubbling.

2 mugs of pasta shapes
¼ x 1 kg bag frozen chopped spinach, thawed
400 g/1 large can tomatoes, chopped
200 g/1 small can sweetcorn
½ tsp dried oregano
Salt and pepper
Grated Parmesan-style cheese

1 Cook the pasta according to the packet directions, drain and return to the pan.

2 Squeeze out the spinach to remove excess moisture. Mix with the pasta, tomatoes, sweetcorn, oregano and seasoning to taste. Heat through until piping hot.

3 Pile the pasta on warm plates and sprinkle with grated cheese. Serve hot.

Chick pea pasta

Any kind of pasta shapes will do for this, which is great when you have very little left in your cupboard – or your pocket. It also works cold as a salad if you have any left over.

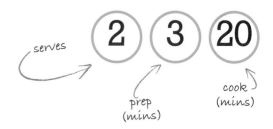

serves **2** 3 20
prep (mins)
cook (mins)

1 Cook the pasta and carrots in boiling salted water for 10 minutes until just tender. Drain.

2 Heat the oil and fry the onion for 4 minutes until soft and golden.

3 Return the pasta and carrots to the pan with the remaining ingredients and heat through for a few minutes until hot. Season with salt and pepper.

4 large handfuls of pasta shapes
1 carrot, sliced
Salt and pepper
1 tbsp oil
1 onion, chopped
½ mug passata or chopped canned tomatoes
1 tbsp tomato purée
½ tsp sugar
425 g/1 large can chick peas, drained
½ tsp dried mixed herbs

Corn fritters with **peanut sauce**

serves **2-4** prep (mins) **10** cook (mins) **10**

You can serve the fritters with bought sweet chilli sauce for a change. If eating alone, make half the quantity, using a small can of sweetcorn and use the rest of the coconut milk for another dish, like one of the Thai curries.

FOR THE SAUCE
400 g/1 large can coconut milk
5 tbsp peanut butter
2 tsp sugar
1/4 tsp chilli powder
1 tsp vinegar or lemon juice
1/2 tsp garlic from a jar or tube
FOR THE FRITTERS
6 tbsp plain flour
2 eggs
4 tbsp milk
300 g/1 medium can sweetcorn, drained
Salt and pepper
Oil
SERVE WITH
Sticks of raw vegetables

1 Put all the ingredients for the sauce in a pan and heat through gently, stirring occasionally, until the sauce boils. Turn off the heat.

2 To make the fritters, put the flour in a bowl. Beat together the eggs and milk, then gradually add to the flour, beating well until smooth.

3 Add the drained sweetcorn and a little seasoning. Mix well.

4 Heat about 5 mm of oil in a large frying pan, and fry spoonfuls of the corn batter for a few minutes until golden on the base. Turn and fry on the other side. Drain on kitchen paper.

5 Reheat the sauce, stirring all the time.

6 Serve the fritters with the hot sauce and sticks of raw vegetables.

Tortilla

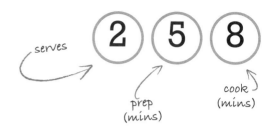

This can be made with leftover cooked potato. Tortilla is delicious served hot or cold with salad. It is the original Spanish omelette but you could add some sliced peppers or courgettes to the mixture for added colour and flavour.

1 tbsp oil
1 large potato, thinly sliced
1 small onion, chopped
Salt and pepper
4 eggs, beaten

1 Heat the oil in a frying pan, add the potato and onion and fry for 4 minutes, stirring, until the potato and onions are really soft.

2 Add a little seasoning and the eggs. Cook gently, lifting and stirring at first, until the egg has almost set.

3 Place under a hot grill to brown and set the top. Serve cut into wedges.

Piperade

 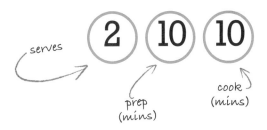
This is basically scrambled eggs with tomatoes and peppers, which is delicious hot or cold. You could use the same principle with a sliced courgette or some mushrooms instead of the pepper. Just use what you have in the kitchen.

1 tbsp oil
Knob of butter or margarine
1 onion, sliced
1 red or green pepper, sliced
4 large tomatoes, quartered
½ tsp garlic from a jar or tube
4 eggs, beaten
Salt and pepper
SERVE WITH
Crusty bread

1 Heat the oil and butter or margarine in a large frying pan. Add the prepared vegetables and garlic and fry gently for about 5 minutes, stirring, until just softened.

2 Add the eggs, season and cook, stirring gently until set and lightly scrambled.

3 Serve straight from the pan with crusty bread.

One-step
ratatouille

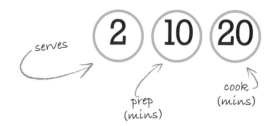

serves **2** **10** **20**

prep (mins)

cook (mins)

This is a Mediterranean vegetable stew, good hot or cold. For non veggies, try it with grilled bacon, sausages, fish, chicken or chops. Try adding a few black or green olives and crumbled Feta cheese on top instead of the grated cheese.

1 small <u>aubergine</u>, sliced

3 <u>courgettes</u>, sliced

1 <u>onion</u>, sliced

1 <u>pepper</u>, sliced

3 tbsp <u>oil</u>

400 g/1 large can <u>tomatoes</u>

1 tbsp <u>tomato purée</u>

½ tsp <u>dried oregano</u>

Large pinch of <u>sugar</u>

<u>Salt and pepper</u>

SERVE WITH

<u>Pasta</u> or <u>bread</u> and grated

<u>Parmesan-style</u> or <u>Cheddar</u>

<u>cheese</u>

1 Put the prepared vegetables in a large pan with the oil and stir over a high heat to soften slightly.

2 Add the canned tomatoes and break up with a wooden spoon. Add the oregano and season with salt and pepper. Cover and simmer for 15 minutes, stirring occasionally, until the vegetables are just tender, no more.

3 Serve with cooked pasta or bread and grated Parmesan-style or Cheddar cheese.

Quick pan pizza

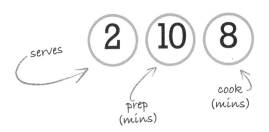

serves **2** prep (mins) **10** cook (mins) **8**

When you fancy a pizza, this is a great quick way to make one. Okay, you have to have some self-raising flour but that will keep for months in the cupboard. Alternatively, you can use a ready-made base.

FOR THE BASE
1 mug self-raising flour (or plain flour and 2 tsp baking powder)
Pinch of salt
3 tbsp oil
About 3 tbsp water

FOR THE TOPPING
2 tbsp tomato purée
1-2 tomatoes, sliced
Large pinch of dried oregano
Large handful of Cheddar cheese, grated

ADDITIONAL TOPPINGS
Chopped ham, sliced mushrooms, drained sweetcorn, diced green or red peppers, pepperami, drained pineapple pieces, sliced olives

1 Mix the flour and salt in a bowl and add 2 tbsp of the oil. Mixing with a knife, gradually work in the water a tablespoon at a time to form a soft but not sticky dough. The amount you use will vary depending on the brand of flour.

2 Squeeze gently into a ball, then flatten out to a round to fit the base of a frying pan.

3 Heat the remaining oil in the frying pan, add the base and fry for about 3 minutes until golden brown underneath. Turn over. Meanwhile, preheat the grill.

4 Spread the tomato purée over the base. Lay the tomato slices on top. Sprinkle with the oregano, add any additional toppings of your choice and top with cheese.

5 Fry for 2–3 minutes, then place the pan under the grill and cook for a few minutes until the cheese is melted and bubbling. Serve hot.

Curried bean & rice salad

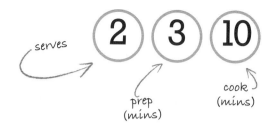

serves 2

prep (mins) 3

cook (mins) 10

Use the rest of the beans to have on toast the next morning or lunchtime (small cans cost more). This is also a good way to use up rice when you've cooked too much for another meal (or just cook more deliberately and use it for this dish).

½ mug long-grain rice
Salt and pepper
½ x 400 g/large can baked beans
1 tsp curry powder
2 tsp mayonnaise or salad cream
Small handful of sultanas
Small chunk of Cheddar, Edam or any cheese, cubed
SERVE WITH
Lettuce leaves

1 Cook the rice in plenty of boiling salted water for 10 minutes, or according to packet directions, until tender. Drain, rinse with cold water and drain again.

2 Place in a bowl. Add the beans, curry powder, mayonnaise or salad cream, sultanas and cheese. Season with pepper and toss well.

3 Serve piled on a bed of lettuce.

Black bean vegetable stir-fry

serves **2** prep (mins) **10** cook (mins) **7**

Ring the changes with any vegetables you have – a chunk of cucumber, cut in matchsticks, instead of the courgette, cauliflower or a little shredded cabbage instead of broccoli. Store black bean sauce in the fridge after opening.

1 tbsp <u>sunflower oil</u>
½ tsp <u>garlic</u> from a jar or tube
1 small <u>onion</u>, sliced
1 <u>red</u> or <u>green pepper</u>, diced
1 <u>carrot</u>, cut in matchsticks
1 <u>courgette</u>, sliced
1 small head of <u>broccoli</u>, cut in tiny florets
425 g/1 large can <u>black beans</u>, drained
1 tbsp <u>black bean sauce</u>
1 tbsp <u>soy sauce</u>
1 tbsp <u>wine, cider, fruit juice</u> or water
SERVE WITH
<u>Rice</u> or <u>Chinese egg noodles</u>

1 Heat the oil in a wok or large frying pan. Add the garlic, onion, pepper and carrot and stir-fry for 2 minutes.

2 Add the courgette and broccoli and stir-fry for a further 3 minutes.

3 Add the beans, sauces and wine or other liquid and toss for 2 minutes until piping hot.

4 Serve on its own or with rice or noodles.

Spaghetti
with pesto

serves   1   5   12

prep
(mins)

cook
(mins)

You can just stir the pesto into the spaghetti and leave out the mushroom bit. To save washing up, cook the spaghetti, drain it in a colander, then cook the mushrooms and onions in the same pan. Return the spaghetti and continue.

¹/₆–¹/₄ x 500 g packet spaghetti
Knob of butter or margarine
4 mushrooms, sliced
1 small onion, finely chopped
2 tsp pesto
SERVE WITH
Grated Parmesan-style cheese
and a tomato salad

1 Cook the spaghetti in boiling water with a pinch of salt for 10 minutes, or according to packet directions, until just tender. Drain and return to the saucepan.

2 Meanwhile, melt the butter or margarine in a frying pan, add the mushrooms and onion and cook for 3–4 minutes until soft and lightly golden.

3 Add the mushroom mixture to the pasta with the pesto and lift and stir lightly over a gentle heat until every strand is coated.

4 Pile into a bowl and serve with Parmesan-style cheese and a tomato salad.

Greek-style salad

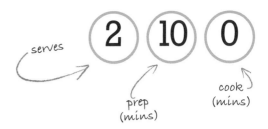

serves **2**

prep (mins) **10**

cook (mins) **0**

You can serve this as a tasty vegetarian meal on its own with lots of crusty bread or pittas, or in smaller portions as an accompaniment to Greek-style lamb (page 129) or grilled or fried chops, chicken or kebabs.

¼ small <u>white cabbage</u>, shredded

¼ <u>iceberg lettuce</u>, shredded

2–4 <u>tomatoes</u>, quartered and sliced

10 cm/4 in piece of <u>cucumber</u>, diced

12 <u>black olives</u>

1 small <u>onion</u>, sliced and separated into rings (see page 20)

½ block <u>Feta cheese</u>, cut into small pieces

½ tsp <u>dried oregano</u>

1 tbsp chopped <u>fresh parsley</u> or <u>coriander</u> (optional)

<u>Salt and pepper</u>

3 tbsp <u>olive</u> or <u>sunflower oil</u>

1 tbsp <u>red wine vinegar</u>

1 Put the shredded cabbage and lettuce on a shallow serving platter.

2 Scatter the tomatoes, cucumber, olives, onion and cheese over the top.

3 Sprinkle with the oregano, parsley or coriander, if using, and some salt and pepper.

4 Trickle the oil and vinegar all over the surface and leave to stand for 30 minutes before serving.

Chicken & turkey meals

Chicken and turkey are more economical than most other meats. Look out at your fresh meat counter for turkey steaks (often on special offer) or buy packs of six frozen fillets, which are excellent value. Chicken thighs are much cheaper than drumsticks or portions and taste just as good. Stir-fry strips, diced and minced poultry are also good buys. Always make sure frozen chicken is thoroughly defrosted before cooking.

TIP A small frozen chicken will easily serve 4. To divide it into portions, before or after cooking, cut the bird in half straight through the breastbone lengthways, cutting right through the back bone. Then divide each half into quarters behind the leg and thigh so you have two breast and wing portions and two leg and thigh portions.

Chicken & corn chowder

serves 2 prep (mins) 2 cook (mins) 4

When you haven't got time to prepare anything from scratch, this makes a tasty, substantial meal. You could, of course, use cooked leftover potatoes if you have some or throw in some leftover cooked rice instead.

300 g/1 medium can <u>condensed cream of chicken soup</u>

<u>Milk</u>

200 g/1 small can <u>sweetcorn</u>

300 g/1 medium can <u>new potatoes</u>, drained and diced

Pinch of <u>chilli powder</u>

SERVE WITH

<u>Crusty bread</u>

1 Empty the soup into a saucepan. Fill the empty soup can with milk and gradually blend it in.

2 Add the contents of the can of sweetcorn, including any liquid, and the diced potatoes, then season with the chilli powder.

3 Heat through gently, stirring occasionally until almost boiling.

4 Serve in soup bowls with crusty bread.

Tandoori chicken

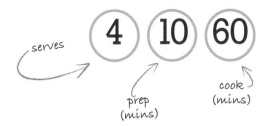

serves **4** prep (mins) **10** cook (mins) **60**

As you need to use the oven, it's not worth cooking less than this quantity. It will keep in the fridge to eat cold or reheat in the microwave. Alternatively, invite friends round to impress them with your culinary skills!

4 large chicken portions
1 mug plain yoghurt
½ tsp garlic from a jar or tube
1 tbsp tandoori powder or paste
1 tsp chopped fresh coriander (optional)
Salt and pepper
Shredded lettuce and wedges of lemon, cucumber and tomato, to garnish
SERVE WITH
Naan breads or oven-cooked rice (see page 18) and mango chutney

1 Pull off as much skin as possible from the chicken. Make several slashes in the flesh. Mix the remaining ingredients, apart from the garnish, together in a large, shallow dish. Add the chicken and rub the mixture well into the slits. When well-coated, leave to marinate in the fridge for at least 3 hours (or all day if you have lectures).

2 Preheat the oven to 200°C/400°F/gas 6/fan oven 180°C. Place the chicken in a baking tin and spoon any remaining marinade over. Cover with foil. Bake in the oven for 30 minutes.

3 Remove the foil from the chicken, pour off any liquid and return to the oven to cook, uncovered, for a further 15 minutes or until well browned and cooked through.

4 Transfer the chicken to warm plates. Garnish with shredded lettuce, and wedges of lemon, cucumber and tomato, and serve with naan breads or rice and mango chutney.

almost finished

Honey & lemon chicken

serves **2**
prep (mins) **3**
cook (mins) **20**

You can vary the flavour by using dried mint, basil, oregano or rosemary instead of the mixed herbs or try adding a little garlic from a jar or tube to the basting mixture. The result has a lovely sweet-sour combination.

2 chicken portions
2 tbsp oil
Salt and pepper
½ tsp dried mixed herbs
3 tbsp lemon juice
1 tbsp clear honey
SERVE WITH
Sautéed potatoes and green beans

1 Rub the chicken with a little of the oil, then season with salt and pepper.

2 Grill the chicken for about 7–8 minutes each side until the skin is crispy and the flesh is almost cooked through.

3 Whisk together the remaining oil, the herbs, lemon juice and honey. Brush or spoon over the chicken, coating the skin completely, and continue to grill, skin-side up, for another 3–4 minutes until a rich golden brown and thoroughly cooked. Coat again after 2 minutes.

4 Serve with sautéed potatoes and green beans.

Chicken & mushroom **risotto**

serves 1-2

prep (mins) 5

cook (mins) 23

This is one dish that really benefits from the fresh basil leaves thrown in at the end but, if you haven't any, add a pinch of dried basil when cooking. Using long-grain rice instead of risotto rice isn't authentic but it's easier and cheaper.

1 chicken stock cube

1½ mugs boiling water

Knob of butter or margarine

1 small onion, finely chopped

1 skinless chicken breast, cut into small pieces

4 mushrooms, sliced

½ mug long-grain rice

2 tbsp double cream

Salt and pepper

2 tbsp grated Parmesan-style cheese

3–4 fresh basil leaves

1 Dissolve the chicken stock cube in a mug of the boiling water.

2 Melt the butter or margarine in a saucepan. Add the onion, chicken and mushrooms and fry over a fairly high heat, stirring, for 3 minutes until the onion is golden and the chicken is almost cooked.

3 Stir in the rice until glistening.

4 Stir in the stock and remaining water. Bring to the boil, stir, turn down the heat as low as possible, cover with a lid, plate or foil and cook for 15–20 minutes until just tender and slightly creamy, stirring once or twice.

5 Stir in the cream, season to taste and add the cheese and basil leaves. Serve straight away.

Crunchy
turkey steaks

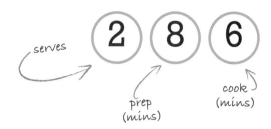

serves **2**

prep (mins) **8**

cook (mins) **6**

This dish is equally good made with boneless pork steaks or chicken breasts, and you can experiment with other stuffing mixes to give a slightly different flavour. If you have any lemon juice, sprinkle a little over before serving.

2 small turkey steaks
1 egg, beaten
½ small packet of sage and onion stuffing mix
1 tbsp oil
SERVE WITH
Mashed potatoes (see page 16)
and green beans

1 Put a turkey steak in a plastic bag. Beat with a rolling pin or bottle to flatten. Repeat with the other piece.

2 Dip the turkey in the beaten egg, then in the stuffing mix to coat completely.

3 Heat enough oil to just coat the base of a frying pan and fry the steaks for about 3 minutes on each side until golden and cooked through. Drain on kitchen paper.

4 Serve with mashed potatoes and green beans.

Quick chicken chow **mein**

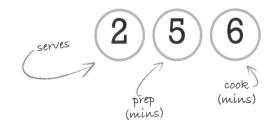

serves **2** **5** **6**

prep (mins)

cook (mins)

You can use a packet of fresh stir-fry vegetables if you prefer – look out for basic economy ranges or ones reduced for quick sale (which should be used on day of purchase or popped in the freezer until ready to use during that week).

1 Cook the noodles according the packet directions.

2 Meanwhile, heat the oil in a large pan or wok. Add the remaining ingredients and stir-fry for 5 minutes.

3 Stir in the noodles, reheat and serve.

1 slab Chinese egg noodles
1 tbsp oil
175 g turkey or chicken stir-fry meat
425 g/1 large can stir-fry mixed vegetables, drained
½ tsp garlic from a jar or tube
1 tbsp soy sauce
1 tbsp vinegar
1 tsp ground ginger
1 tbsp sugar

Chicken & coconut masala

serves **2**   prep (mins) **8**   cook (mins) **12**

Why not grow a pot of fresh coriander on the kitchen windowsill? It's much nicer than using dried, if you can. Put a few leaves in a cup and chop with scissors, then throw them in at the last moment for a really authentic flavour.

175 g diced chicken or turkey meat
1 small onion, chopped
1 small green pepper, sliced (optional)
2 tsp mild curry powder or paste
1 tbsp oil
1 mug boiling water
1 chicken stock cube
½ packet of creamed coconut
Small handful of raisins
Salt and pepper
SERVE WITH
Plain boiled rice

1 Fry the chicken, onion, pepper and curry powder or paste in the oil for 4 minutes, stirring.

2 Add the remaining ingredients. Bring to the boil, then reduce the heat and simmer for about 6 minutes until the chicken is cooked, stirring several times.

3 If the sauce is still a little runny, remove the chicken with a draining spoon and boil the sauce rapidly, stirring, until it has reduced and thickened, then return the chicken to the sauce. Season to taste, if necessary.

4 Serve on a bed of rice.

Lightly spiced chicken **casserole**

serves **2**

prep (mins) **10**

cook (mins) **60**

It's worth using the oven if you cook a main course and a rice accompaniment. If you prefer, you can simmer the chicken in a saucepan on the hob instead but do stir it occasionally to prevent sticking, and serve with boiled rice.

2 chicken portions
1 tbsp plain flour
Salt and pepper
Large knob of butter or margarine
1 tsp garam masala or curry powder
300 g/1 medium can condensed cream of mushroom soup
SERVE WITH
Oven-cooked rice (see page 18) and a green vegetable

1 Preheat the oven to 180°C/350°F/gas 4/fan oven 160°C.

2 Wipe the chicken with kitchen paper. Mix the flour with a little salt and pepper and use to coat the chicken.

3 Melt the butter or margarine in a flameproof casserole and fry the chicken on all sides for about 4 minutes to brown. Alternatively, use a frying pan and then transfer to an ovenproof casserole.

4 Drain off all but 1 tbsp of the fat. Stir in the garam masala or curry powder, then blend in the soup.

5 Cook in the oven for 1 hour or until the chicken is tender and cooked through.

6 Serve with oven-cooked rice and a green vegetable, such as broccoli.

Baked chicken in **tomato sauce**

serves **2** prep (mins) **10** cook (mins) **60**

If you don't have a flameproof casserole, do the browning in the frying pan, then put the mixture in an ovenproof dish and cover it with foil to cook in the oven at the same time as the potatoes. Add some mushrooms if you like.

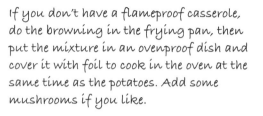

1 onion, chopped
1 tbsp oil
2 chicken portions
Salt and pepper
300 g/1 medium can condensed tomato soup
½ tsp dried basil
SERVE WITH
Jacket or roast potatoes (see page 16) and salad

1 Preheat the oven to 180°C/350°F/gas 4/fan oven 160°C.

2 In a flameproof casserole or frying pan, fry the onion in the oil for 2 minutes. Add the chicken, skin-side down, and fry for 2 minutes to brown.

3 Turn the chicken skin-side up, sprinkle with salt and pepper and spoon the soup over. Add the basil. If using a frying pan, transfer the chicken to a casserole, stir the soup into the pan juices, then spoon over.

4 Cover and cook for 1 hour or until the chicken is tender. Stir occasionally and add a little water if necessary.

5 Serve with jacket or roast potatoes and salad.

Grilled chicken with garlic

serves **2** prep (mins) **2** cook (mins) **20**

This sauce can also be served with fish or vegetables so it is very versatile. You can fry the chicken in a little oil, if you prefer, then remove and keep warm, pour off the excess oil and make the sauce in the same pan.

2 chicken portions or large thighs

Oil

Salt and pepper

2 tsp cornflour

½ mug milk

Knob of butter or margarine

¼ x 200 g/1 small carton garlic and herb soft cheese

SERVE WITH

Pasta and a green salad

1 Smear the chicken pieces with oil and season lightly with salt and pepper. Grill for about 20 minutes, turning occasionally until crisp, golden and cooked through.

2 Meanwhile, whisk the cornflour with a little of the milk in a saucepan until smooth. Stir in the remaining milk. Add the butter or margarine.

3 Bring to the boil, stirring until thickened. Add the cheese in small pieces and continue stirring over a gentle heat until blended. Season the sauce with salt and pepper.

4 Transfer the chicken to warm plates and spoon the sauce over. Serve with pasta and a green salad.

Chicken & vegetable stir-fry

serves **2** prep (mins) **10** cook (mins) **7**

If eating alone, simply reheat or eat it cold the next day. Use other veggies like carrots, courgettes and cucumber, cut in matchsticks, or shredded cabbage or pak choi (add greens with the mushrooms) or ready-prepared stir-fry veggies.

½ x 250 g pack rice noodles
1 tbsp sunflower oil
1 onion, cut in wedges and separated into layers
½ tsp garlic from a jar or tube
1 tsp grated root ginger from a jar or use ground
1 green pepper, thinly sliced
1 red pepper, thinly sliced
2 boneless chicken thighs, cut in thin strips
4 mushrooms, sliced
2–3 tbsp soy sauce
A little apple juice or water

1 Reconstitute the rice noodles in boiling water according to the packet directions.

2 Heat the oil and stir-fry the onions, garlic, ginger, peppers and chicken for 4 minutes until the chicken is cooked.

3 Add the mushrooms and stir-fry for 1–2 minutes.

4 Add the soy sauce and a little apple juice or water to moisten. Stir-fry for a further 30 seconds.

5 Drain the rice noodles and put in bowls, then spoon the chicken mixture over and serve.

Thai green chicken curry

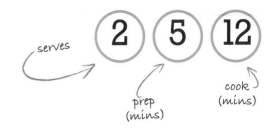

serves **2** prep (mins) **5** cook (mins) **12**

Vary the vegetable by using little broccoli or cauliflower florets or sliced courgettes instead of beans. You can use about 175 g of chicken stir-fry meat instead of the breasts.

1 tbsp <u>oil</u>
1 small <u>onion</u>, chopped
2 <u>skinless chicken breasts</u>, cubed
1 tbsp <u>Thai green curry paste</u>
½ x 400 g/1 large can <u>coconut milk</u>
½ mug <u>frozen green beans</u>, cut into short lengths
<u>Salt and pepper</u>
SERVE WITH
<u>Boiled rice</u>

1 Heat the oil and fry the onion and chicken, stirring, for 2 minutes.

2 Stir in the curry paste and add the coconut milk and beans.

3 Bring to the boil, reduce the heat, part-cover and simmer gently for about 10 minutes until the chicken is tender and cooked through.

4 Taste and season, if necessary.

5 Serve with boiled rice in bowls.

TIP Store the rest of the coconut milk in a covered container in the fridge and use within 3 days for another dish, or mix it with a mashed banana and some fruit juice for a great breakfast pick-me-up (or purée with a blender if you have one).

One-step
roast chicken

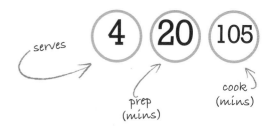

serves **4** **20** **105**
prep (mins)
cook (mins)

Most supermarket birds don't have the giblets inside but do check! Use as many vegetables as you like. I allow 4 pieces each of potato, carrot and parsnip and 1–2 small onions per person.

1.2 kg/2¾ lb small <u>roasting chicken</u>, thawed if frozen
5 ml/1 tsp <u>dried mixed herbs</u>
<u>Oil</u>
<u>Salt</u>
4 <u>potatoes</u>, scrubbed and cut into even sized pieces
4 <u>carrots</u>, peeled and cut into chunky fingers
1 large <u>parsnip</u>, peeled and cut into chunky fingers
4–8 small <u>onions</u>, peeled but left whole
1 tbsp <u>plain flour</u>
1 <u>chicken</u> or <u>vegetable stock cube</u>
<u>Pepper</u>
SERVE WITH
<u>Peas</u> or <u>beans</u> (optional)

1 Preheat the oven to 190°C/375°F/gas 5/fan oven 170°C.

2 Wipe inside and out of the bird with kitchen paper and pull off any excess fat from the body cavity. (You can feel it just inside the opening if there is any.)

3 Put the herbs in the body cavity, then place the bird in a large roasting tin. Rub all over with oil and a little salt.

4 Boil the potatoes, carrots and parsnips in plenty of salted water. Cook for 3 minutes, then drain, reserving a mugful of the cooking water.

5 Arrange all the vegetables around the chicken and drizzle with oil, then toss to coat completely. Sprinkle with a little salt.

almost finished

6 Roast in the oven for 1½ hours or until the chicken and vegetables are golden and cooked through, turning the vegetables once or twice during cooking. Transfer the chicken to a plate and the vegetables to a warm dish and keep warm.

7 Mix the flour with a little cold water until smooth, then blend in the reserved vegetable water. Stir into the juices in the roasting tin and crumble in the stock cube. Bring to the boil, stirring. Cut up the chicken and serve with the vegetables and gravy.

Curried chicken mayonnaise

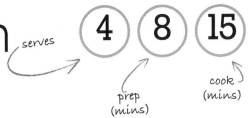

serves **4** **8** **15**

prep (mins) cook (mins)

This is a great way of using up cooked chicken and it makes a little chicken go a long way. It's a great dish if friends are coming round. You can prepare it in advance then keep it in the fridge until you are ready to eat.

1 packet of savoury rice with mushrooms
½ small cooked chicken
3 tbsp mayonnaise
4 tsp mango chutney
2 tsp curry paste
SERVE WITH
Popadoms

1 Cook the savoury rice according to the packet directions. Drain, spoon into a ring on a large serving plate and leave until cold.

2 Pick all the meat off the chicken and cut into bite sized pieces.

3 Mix the mayonnaise with the chutney and curry paste. Fold in the chicken and pile into the centre of the cold rice.

4 Serve with lots of popadoms.

Curried chicken & potato salad

serves **2** prep (mins) **5** cook (mins) **0**

This is an easy version of coronation chicken and a great way to use up leftover chicken. Or you can substitute turkey, pork, even prawns. Canned potatoes sound a bit odd but they are okay in the dressing.

1 Mix together the mayonnaise, curry paste and chutney, then stir in the chicken.

2 Put the spring onions, potatoes and cucumber in a separate bowl. Add the oil, vinegar, salt, pepper and toss gently.

3 Spoon the potato salad on to plates and top with the chicken mayonnaise.

2 tbsp mayonnaise
1 tsp curry paste
2 tsp mango chutney or sweet pickle
1 cooked chicken portion, diced
2 spring onions, chopped
300 g/1 medium can new potatoes, drained and quartered or a handful of freshly boiled ones (see page 15)
5 cm/2 in piece of cucumber, diced
1 tbsp oil
1 tsp vinegar
Salt and pepper

Turkey
stroganoff

You can use chicken, pork or thin strips of frying steak instead of turkey for this dish if you prefer. I also like it with about ¼ tsp coarsely crushed black peppercorns added to the meat before frying.

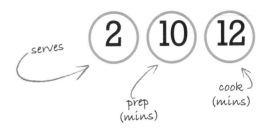

serves 2
prep (mins) 10
cook (mins) 12

Knob of butter or margarine
1 small onion, sliced
4 mushrooms, sliced
175 g turkey stir-fry meat
1 tbsp wine, beer or cider
½ mug (or a small carton) plain yoghurt or crème fraîche
Salt and pepper
SERVE WITH
Tagliatelle and a green salad

1   Melt the butter or margarine and fry the onion and mushrooms for 3 minutes.

2   Add the turkey and fry for 4–5 minutes until cooked through.

3   Stir in the wine, beer or cider and bubble briefly.

4   Stir in the yoghurt or crème fraîche and heat through but do not boil. Season to taste.

5   Serve with tagliatelle and a green salad.

Meat
meals

Most meat is fairly expensive. Mince is not only a good buy but also very versatile. Large packs of free flow beef, lamb or pork mince are ideal as you can use as little or as much as you need – and you can use it from frozen. Some cuts of pork – such as belly slices or shoulder steaks – won't mean taking out a mortgage, and thin frying steaks are quite a good buy. Good-quality sausages make a great meal but, as I've said before, avoid the economy ranges as they'll be full of fat, rusk and not a lot of decent meat.

Liver and kidneys are really good for you and cook in no time. I've included a recipe for each in the hopes of tempting you. I guarantee you'll be pleasantly surprised. I've also included corned beef as it's a great standby to keep in the cupboard (it makes great toasted sandwiches too, mashed with tomato ketchup or brown sauce

Homemade
chunky burgers

serves

(2) (5) (12)

prep
(mins)

cook
(mins)

If you buy fresh mince and you don't need it all, divide it into portion sizes, wrap each separately in plastic bags or tightly in foil, label (so you remember what it is) and freeze. Add a pinch of dried mixed herbs if you like.

225 g/2 mugs minced beef, lamb, pork or turkey, thawed, if frozen
1 small onion, chopped
½ tsp mustard
½ tsp tomato purée
1 tsp Worcestershire sauce
Salt and pepper
1 small egg, beaten
SERVE WITH
Burger buns and salad

1 Mix together the meat, onion, mustard, tomato purée and Worcestershire sauce, seasoning to taste with salt and pepper.

2 Bind the mixture with the egg (you might not need to use all of it, in which case keep it in the fridge for a piece of eggy bread (see page 48) for breakfast or a snack next day). Shape into 2 burgers and chill (if time) before cooking.

3 Grill for about 6 minutes on each side, depending on the thickness, until cooked through.

4 Serve in burger buns with salad.

Meat loaf

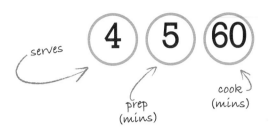

serves 4 · prep (mins) 5 · cook (mins) 60

This is worth making and keeping the remainder (when cold) well wrapped in foil in the fridge. You can slice it and put it in hunks of French bread or serve it on a plate with salad and pickles.

350 g/3 mugs minced beef, lamb, pork or turkey
½ packet of sage and onion stuffing mix
2 tbsp tomato purée
2 tbsp water
Salt and pepper
1 small egg, beaten
SERVE WITH
Canned tomatoes, crusty bread or salad and pickles

1. Preheat the oven to 180°C/350°F/gas 4/fan oven 160°C. Grease a 450 g loaf tin or deep ovenproof dish.

2. Mix together all the ingredients and press into the tin. Cover with foil and bake in the oven for 1 hour. Alternatively put the covered tin or dish in a large frying pan. Surround as deep as possible with boiling water. Cover the whole thing with more foil and cook over a low heat so it bubbles gently, for 1 hour until firm. Check occasionally to make sure it doesn't boil dry and add more boiling water if necessary.

3. Cool slightly, then turn out, if in a tin.

4. Cut in thick slices, or cut into pieces if in a dish, and serve hot with canned tomatoes, green beans and crusty bread or potatoes.

Quick beef pasta

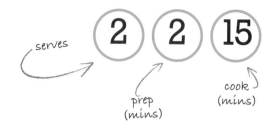

serves **2**

prep (mins) **2**

cook (mins) **15**

It's better to cook meat from scratch than use cans – you know exactly what you're getting. But canned minced steak does make a tasty pasta dish and is great when you need something quick and cheap. Choose a good quality brand.

1 mug <u>pasta shapes</u>
175 g/1 small can <u>minced</u>
<u>steak with onions</u>
½ tsp <u>dried mixed herbs</u>
Large handful of <u>grated</u>
<u>Cheddar cheese</u>
1–2 <u>tomatoes</u>, sliced (optional)
SERVE WITH
<u>Salad</u>

1 Cook the pasta according to the packet directions. Drain in a colander.

2 Return to the saucepan, add the mince and season with the herbs.

3 Heat through, stirring gently, until piping hot.

4 Turn on to warm plates and sprinkle the cheese over the top.

5 Arrange the tomato slices around, if using, and serve with salad.

Spaghetti bolognese

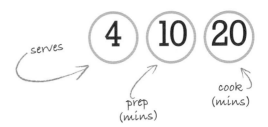

Make this quantity of sauce as it keeps well in the fridge for several days. You need ⅙–¼ x 500 g packet of spaghetti per person. To make the sauce serve more, cook extra pasta and mix it with the sauce rather than spooning it on top.

350 g/3 mugs minced beef or lamb
1 onion, chopped
½ tsp garlic from a jar or tube
400 g/1 large can tomatoes, chopped
1 tbsp tomato purée
Salt and pepper
1 tsp dried oregano
Pinch of sugar
¾–1 x 500 g packet of spaghetti (depending on appetites), or about ⅙–¼ if eating alone
Parmesan-style cheese, grated

1 Put the meat, onion and garlic in a saucepan. Cook, stirring, until the grains of meat are brown and separate.

2 Add the remaining ingredients except the spaghetti and cheese. Stir well. Bring to the boil, reduce the heat, half-cover and simmer gently for 15–20 minutes until a rich sauce has formed. Stir gently occasionally. Taste and re-season if necessary.

3 Meanwhile, cook the spaghetti according to the packet directions. Drain and pile on to serving plates. Spoon the sauce over and top with Parmesan-style cheese.

Lasagne
al forno

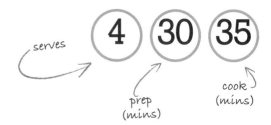

serves **4** · prep (mins) **30** · cook (mins) **35**

If you make this for friends, get a garlic baguette and put it in the oven to cook with the lasagne for the last 15 minutes. Otherwise this can be made then kept in the fridge and a portion reheated in the microwave over the next few days

Bolognese sauce (as for Spaghetti Bolognese, page 115)
6 tbsp plain flour
2 mugs milk
Large knob of butter or margarine
½ tsp dried mixed herbs
Salt and pepper
3–4 tbsp grated Parmesan-style cheese
About 8 sheets of no-need-to-precook lasagne
SERVE WITH
Garlic bread and green salad

1. Make the Bolognese sauce (see page 115).

2. While it's cooking, make the white sauce. Mix the flour and milk in a saucepan, using a metal whisk, until smooth. Add the butter or margarine and herbs. Bring to the boil and cook for 2 minutes, stirring with the whisk all the time until thick and smooth. Stir in half the cheese, and season to taste.

3. Preheat the oven to 190°C/375°F/gas 5/fan oven 170°C.

4. Spoon just a little of the Bolognese sauce into a large shallow ovenproof dish, then cover with a layer of lasagne sheets. Layer the meat thinly with lasagne until all the meat is used, finishing with a layer of lasagne.

5. Spoon the sauce over the top. Sprinkle with the remaining cheese.

6. Bake in the oven for 35 minutes or until golden brown and bubbling and the lasagne feels tender when a knife is inserted down through the centre.

almost finished

7. Serve hot with the garlic bread and green salad.

Chilli con carne

serves 2 5 20
prep (mins) cook (mins)

Make it serve an extra couple of people by adding an extra can of red kidney beans and tomatoes. You can adjust the chilli to taste. This is a great party dish as you can make large quantities quite easily and reheat it in a large pan.

1 onion, chopped
½ tsp garlic from a jar or tube
175 g/1 heaped mug minced beef
¼–½ tsp chilli powder
½ tsp ground cumin (optional)
½ tsp dried oregano or mixed herbs
400 g/1 large can tomatoes
425 g/1 large can red kidney beans, drained
1 tbsp tomato purée
Salt and pepper
Pinch of sugar
SERVE WITH
Plain boiled rice or flour tortillas or crispy taco shells, grated Cheddar cheese and shredded lettuce

1 Put the onion, garlic and beef in a pan and cook until brown and the grains of meat are separate.

2 Add the remaining ingredients and break up the tomatoes with a wooden spoon.

3 Bring to the boil, reduce the heat and simmer for 10–15 minutes, stirring occasionally, or until pulpy and a good rich colour (the longer you simmer, the better the flavour).

4 Serve with plain boiled rice, rolled up in flour tortillas or in crispy taco shells with grated cheese and shredded lettuce to sprinkle over.

TIP To make enchiladas, roll up the chilli in flour tortillas, lay them in a flameproof dish, sprinkle with grated cheese and grill until melted and bubbling.

Rich mince with new potatoes

 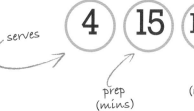
You may as well make enough for four as you can keep it in the fridge if you are eating alone, or pop the rest in the freezer, for up to two weeks. If you prefer, leave out the potatoes and serve with spaghetti.

2 tbsp <u>sunflower oil</u>
2 large <u>onions</u>, chopped
4 mugs <u>minced beef</u> (or a 500 g pack)
2 <u>carrots</u>, chopped
3 tbsp <u>plain flour</u>
3 mugs <u>boiling water</u>
2 <u>beef stock cubes</u>
1 bay leaf or 1 tsp <u>dried mixed herbs</u>
<u>Salt and pepper</u>
450 g <u>baby new potatoes</u>, washed
2 mugs <u>frozen peas</u>

1 Preheat the oven to 160°C/325°F/gas 3/fan oven 140°C.

2 Heat the oil in a flameproof casserole (or use a saucepan and then tip into an ovenproof dish at step 5) and fry the onions, beef and carrots, stirring, over a fairly high heat for about 5 minutes until the meat is no longer pink and all the grains are separate.

3 Stir in the flour then the water and stock cubes and bring to the boil, stirring.

4 Add the bay leaf or mixed herbs, seasoning and the potatoes. Cover with a lid or foil and cook in the oven for 2 hours.

5 Discard the bay leaf, if used, stir in the peas and return to the oven for 15 minutes. Taste and re-season if necessary. Ladle into warm bowls and serve.

TIP I've cooked it in the oven because you can just leave it and go and study or whatever you want to do. You could cook it in a pan on top of the stove, but you'll need to keep it over a very low heat and stir it from time to time. You may need to add a little extra liquid if it gets too thick and it'll only take about an hour to get really tasty.

Keema curry & rice

serves 1-2   5   25
prep (mins)   cook (mins)

This is a mild but tasty curry with just a hint of ginger. If you don't have any in the cupboard, just leave it out. As always, adjust the spices to your own taste.

2 tbsp oil
1 onion, chopped
1 mug minced beef
4 tsp curry powder
½ tsp ground ginger
1 tsp garlic purée
½ mug water
2 tsp tomato purée
Salt
½ mug long-grain rice
SERVE WITH
Naan bread or salad

1 Heat the oil and fry the onion for 4 minutes until soft but not browned.

2 Add the meat and fry, stirring, until no longer pink and all the grains are separate.

3 Stir in the spices and garlic and fry for 3 minutes.

4 Add the water, bring to the boil, cover and simmer gently for 15 minutes, stirring occasionally, until cooked through. Season to taste.

5 Meanwhile, cook the rice in boiling salted water for about 8 minutes until tender. Drain.

6 Serve with naan bread or salad.

Beef hot **pot**

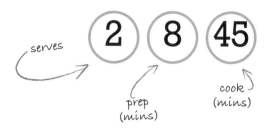

serves **2**   prep (mins) **8**   cook (mins) **45**

I don't advocate using many canned meats but using a good quality can of stewed steak for this dish really tastes as if you've spent hours preparing it! If you don't like crunchy water chestnuts, add some sliced mushrooms instead.

2 large <u>potatoes</u>, thinly sliced
450 g/1 large can <u>stewed steak</u>
225 g/1 small can <u>water chestnuts</u>, drained and sliced
Large pinch of <u>dried oregano</u> or <u>mixed herbs</u>
300 g/1 medium can <u>condensed mushroom soup</u>
2 tbsp <u>water</u>
SERVE WITH
<u>Broccoli</u>

1 Preheat the oven to 200°C/400°F/gas 6/fan oven 180°C.

2 Boil the sliced potatoes in water for 2 minutes. Drain and rinse with cold water.

3 Empty the meat into a shallow ovenproof dish and break up with a wooden spoon.

4 Drain and slice the water chestnuts and scatter over. Sprinkle with the herbs.

5 Spoon over about half the can of soup.

6 Arrange the sliced potatoes neatly in a single layer over the top.

7 Thin the remaining soup slightly with the water and spread over.

8 Bake in the oven for about 45 minutes until the potatoes are cooked and the top is a golden brown.

9 Serve with broccoli.

almost finished

Corned beef fritters

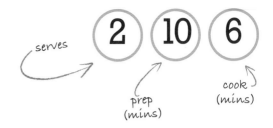

serves 2

prep (mins) 10

cook (mins) 6

Put the potatoes on to cook before you start the fritters. The peas can be cooked quickly while the fritters are frying. This is terribly '70s' but delicious all the same and very popular with the students who tried it!

½ mug plain flour

Salt and pepper

2 eggs, beaten

4 tbsp milk

350 g/1 large can corned beef, cut into 8 slices

Oil, for shallow-frying

SERVE WITH

Tomato relish or ketchup, mashed potatoes (see page 16) or crusty bread and peas

1 Put the flour in a bowl with a little salt and pepper. Add the eggs and milk and beat well.

2 Dip the slices of corned beef in the batter.

3 Heat about 5 mm oil in a frying pan. When hot but not smoking, fry the fritters over a fairly high heat for about 3 minutes on each side until golden brown.

4 Drain on kitchen paper and serve with tomato relish, mashed potatoes and peas.

Potato
moussaka

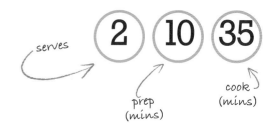

serves **2**

prep (mins) **10**

cook (mins) **35**

The cinnamon gives an authentic Greek flavour and is useful for flavouring lots of things from apples to chocolate. You can use an aubergine instead of potatoes for a more Greek-style dish but they tend to be a bit more expensive than spuds!

2 large <u>potatoes</u>, scrubbed and sliced (not peeled) or a large can of potatoes

2 mugs <u>minced beef</u> or <u>lamb</u>

2 <u>tomatoes</u>, chopped

2 tbsp <u>tomato purée</u>

½ tsp <u>garlic</u> from a jar or tube

½–1 tsp <u>ground cinnamon</u>

½ tsp <u>dried oregano</u>

<u>Salt and pepper</u>

½ mug <u>plain yoghurt</u>

1 <u>egg</u>

Large handful of <u>grated</u>
<u>Cheddar cheese</u>

SERVE WITH

<u>Salad</u>

1 Preheat the oven to 190°C/375°F/gas 5/fan oven 170°C.

2 Boil the potatoes in salted water for about 5 minutes until tender, then drain. If using canned potatoes, drain and slice them.

3 Fry the mince in a pan, stirring until no longer pink and all the grains are separate. Stir in the tomatoes, tomato purée, garlic, cinnamon and oregano. Allow to bubble for 5 minutes, stirring frequently. Season to taste. Layer the potatoes and meat mixture in an ovenproof dish, finishing with a layer of potatoes.

4 Beat the yoghurt with the egg and a little salt and pepper. Stir in the cheese. Spoon over the sliced potato topping.

5 Bake in the oven for about 35 minutes until bubbling, golden and the top has set.

6 Serve with a salad.

Piquant
pan-fried steak

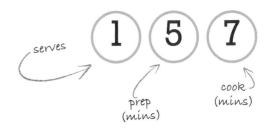

serves

1

prep (mins)

5

cook (mins)

7

Start to cook the potatoes before you begin cooking the steaks. The peas can be cooked in a microwave or boiled for a few minutes towards the end. I've done this for one but you can easily cook enough for 4 people in one large frying pan.

1 thin frying steak

1 tsp lemon juice

Pepper

Knob of butter or margarine

1 tsp oil

1 small onion, finely chopped or grated

1 tsp soy sauce

1 tbsp Worcestershire sauce

A splash of water

SERVE WITH

Sauté potatoes (see page 16) and peas

1 Smear the steak all over with the lemon juice and add a good grinding of pepper. Ideally leave it to marinate in the fridge – even all day – as it makes the steak more tender (but you can cook straight away if necessary).

2 Melt the butter or margarine with the oil in a frying pan. Add the steak and cook over a high heat for about 2 minutes on each side until just cooked through. Remove from the pan and keep warm.

3 Add the onion to the pan and cook, stirring, for 2 minutes until soft.

4 Add the remaining ingredients and allow to bubble for 1 minute, then spoon over the steak.

5 Serve with the sauté potatoes and peas.

Peppered liver with carrot mash

serves **3** prep (mins) **15** cook (mins) **20**

Lamb's liver is cheap but it's sold in packs enough for 3–4 servings. If eating alone, cook it all (halve the mash and sauce), and eat the rest cold, chopped with mayo as a pitta bread filler with lettuce or in a mixed salad.

3–4 large potatoes peeled and cut in small pieces
3–4 carrots, sliced
Salt
350 g pack lamb's liver, thawed if frozen
1 tbsp plain flour
2 tbsp coarsely crushed black peppercorns
2 large knobs of butter or margarine
2 tbsp oil
½ mug red wine or apple juice
1 tbsp tomato purée
1 tsp sugar (if using wine)

1 Boil the potatoes and carrots together in lightly salted water in a part-covered pan until tender.

2 When the vegetables are almost cooked, dry the liver on kitchen paper, cut any thick pieces into thinner slices. Mix the flour and peppercorns and use to coat the liver.

3 Heat a knob of butter or margarine and the oil in a large frying pan. Fry the liver over a high heat on one side for a couple of minutes until browned. Turn and cook just until droplets of juice appear on the surface, no longer. Transfer to a plate.

4 Drain the vegetables, reserving the water. Mash with the remaining knob of butter or margarine. Put the plate of liver over the top and cover with the lid to keep warm.

5 Quickly stir the wine or apple juice, tomato purée and a little salt into the juices in the frying pan. Add the sugar if using wine, and cook, stirring, until bubbling. Thin with a little of the reserved cooking water, if necessary.

6 Pile the mash on plates. Top with the liver and spoon the sauce over.

Devilled
kidneys with rice

serves **2** prep (mins) **15** cook (mins) **17**

Kidneys are cheap and nutritious. Here they're served in a slightly spicy rich sauce and were a traditional Victorian breakfast dish – but I recommend them for supper! They can be reheated a second day but are best served fresh.

¾–1 mug long-grain rice
3 large handfuls of frozen cut beans, peas or mixed vegetables
350 g pack lambs' kidneys
¼ x 250 g tub butter or margarine
4 streaky bacon rashers, rinded and diced (optional)
6 mushrooms, sliced
1 tsp curry paste
1 tsp made English mustard
2 tbsp tomato purée
1 tbsp sugar
2 tbsp water

1 Cook the rice in plenty of boiling, lightly salted water for 4 minutes. Add the vegetables, then boil for a further 4 minutes until the rice is just tender but with some 'bite'. Drain in a colander.

2 Put some water in the saucepan and sit the colander on top. Cover the rice with the saucepan lid and keep warm over a very gentle heat.

3 Hold a kidney one at a time and snip out the white core with scissors, then snip into bite-sized pieces.

4 Put the beans, peas or vegetables on to cook.

5 Heat the butter or margarine in a large frying pan over a fairly high heat. Add the kidneys, bacon, if using, and mushrooms and fry, stirring, for 3 minutes.

6 Add the remaining ingredients and cook over a gentle heat, stirring, for about 4 minutes until the kidneys are cooked through and bathed in sauce. Add a little more water if necessary.

7 Spoon the vegetable rice on to warm plates and top with the kidneys.

Chilli tacos in **minutes**

serves **2** **5** prep (mins) **5** cook (mins)

If you prefer something less fiery, just reduce the amount of chilli and taste as you go. If you want to use fresh mince, fry it with a chopped onion until browned, then add the remaining ingredients.

120 g/1 small can <u>minced steak</u>
2 tsp <u>tomato purée</u>
½ tsp <u>chilli powder</u>
¼ tsp <u>garlic purée</u>
400 g/1 large can <u>red kidney beans</u>, rinsed and drained
6 <u>taco shells</u>
SERVE WITH
Shredded <u>lettuce</u>, chopped <u>tomato</u> and <u>grated cheese</u>

1 Put all the ingredients except the taco shells in a pan and heat through, stirring occasionally, until heated through and bubbling.

2 If you like, warm the taco shells in the microwave or warm oven.

3 Spoon the mixture into the shells.

4 Top with shredded lettuce, chopped tomato and grated cheese.

Corned beef pan **hash**

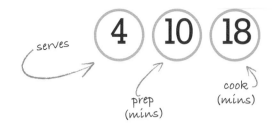

serves 4 · prep (mins) 10 · cook (mins) 18

This is a tasty traditional favourite that is quick to prepare. Use cooked leftover potatoes if you have them. If you hate chopping onions, you can buy frozen diced onion and just use a handful instead of chopping one – it's great!

3–4 potatoes, peeled and diced

1 onion, chopped

1 tbsp oil

350 g/1 large can corned beef, diced

400 g/1 large can baked beans in tomato sauce

1 tbsp brown sauce

Salt and pepper

SERVE WITH

Crusty bread and salad

1 Boil the potatoes in lightly salted water for 3–4 minutes until soft. Drain.

2 Fry the onion in the oil for 3 minutes until soft but not brown.

3 Mix in the remaining ingredients and fry for 5 minutes, turning the mixture occasionally.

4 Press down with a fish slice and continue frying for a further 5 minutes without disturbing until crisp and brown underneath. Loosen the base and invert on to a plate.

5 Serve cut in quarters with crusty bread and salad.

TIP Serve any remaining hash cold in split pitta breads with some shredded salad for a filling lunch or supper.

Broccoli with ham **and cheese**

serves **2** prep (mins) **10** cook (mins) **10**

This is really nice with baked beans or canned tomatoes simply heated up in a saucepan as you pop this under the grill. Or you could slice a couple of tomatoes and arrange them round the top before grilling, instead of the salad.

1 small head <u>broccoli</u>
2 slices of <u>ham</u>
2 tbsp <u>plain flour</u>
Knob of <u>butter</u> or <u>margarine</u>
½ mug <u>milk</u>
½ mug grated <u>Cheddar cheese</u>
<u>Salt and pepper</u>
SERVE WITH
<u>Crusty bread</u> and a <u>sliced</u>
<u>tomato salad</u>

1 Separate the broccoli into florets and cook in boiling salted water for about 5 minutes until just tender.

2 Lay side by side in a buttered ovenproof dish. Top with the ham.

3 Whisk the flour and butter or margarine into the milk in a pan. Bring to the boil and boil for 2 minutes, whisking all the time until thickened and smooth. Stir in most of the cheese and season to taste.

4 Pour the sauce over the broccoli and ham. Sprinkle with the remaining cheese and grill for about 3 minutes or until golden brown.

5 Serve with crusty bread and a tomato salad.

Greek-style roast lamb

serves **3** prep (mins) **10** cook (mins) **240**

Lamb shoulder is an economical cut and slow-cooked tastes fantastic. It's really easy, too! If you were really going to impress your friends, serve some bought hummus or taramasalata with warm pitta breads first as a starter.

½ lean shoulder of lamb, about 700 g
1 tsp garlic from a jar or tube
½ tsp dried oregano
Salt and pepper
3–4 large potatoes, peeled and halved or quartered
¾ mug boiling water
½ chicken stock cube
Some chopped fresh parsley, to garnish (optional)
SERVE WITH
Warm pitta breads and a Greek-style salad (see page 91)

1 Preheat the oven to 150°C/300°F/gas 2/fan oven 130°C.

2 Put the lamb in a fairly large roasting tin. Spread the garlic over and sprinkle with the oregano and a little salt and pepper.

3 Arrange the halved potatoes around and sprinkle with salt. Mix the boiling water and stock cube together and pour around.

4 Cover with a lid or tightly with foil and cook in the oven for 4 hours or until meltingly tender.

5 While it is cooking, make the salad. When about to serve, warm the pitta breads in the oven briefly.

6 Transfer the meat and potatoes to a large plate. Cut all the meat off the bone (it will fall away) and cut into neat pieces. Transfer to warm plates with the potatoes. Spoon the juices over and sprinkle with parsley, if using.

7 Serve with warm pitta breads and a Greek-style salad alongside.

Sheesh kebabs

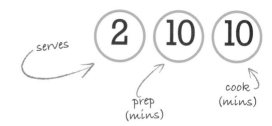

serves **2** prep (mins) **10** cook (mins) **10**

These are easy to make at home. Simply mix the ingredients and shape them round kebab skewers. If you haven't any skewers, just shape the mixture into ovals and grill them. Cook some rice as soon as you start to grill the kebabs.

2 mugs minced lamb, thawed if frozen
1 small onion, grated
1 tsp ground cinnamon
½ tsp ground ginger (optional)
½ tsp ground cumin (optional)
Large pinch of chilli powder (optional)
½ tsp dried oregano
1 tsp lemon juice
1 tbsp plain yoghurt
1 tbsp plain flour, plus extra for dusting
Salt and pepper
Wedges of lemon, to garnish
SERVE WITH
Boiled rice, shredded lettuce, sliced tomatoes, sliced cucumber and mango chutney

1 Put all the ingredients in a bowl with a little salt and pepper and stir and squeeze together until well mixed.

2 Preheat the grill.

3 With wet hands, divide the mixture into 4–6 pieces and shape each piece into a sausage shape around 2 skewers. Lay on foil on the grill rack. Grill for 10 minutes, turning once or twice, until golden brown and cooked through.

4 Put on plates, garnish with lemon wedges, if liked, and serve with rice, lettuce, tomato, cucumber and mango chutney.

Couscous with spiced lamb

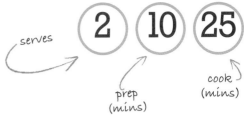

serves **2**
prep (mins) **10**
cook (mins) **25**

This tastes like a North African lamb tagine. If you like dried apricots, add a few, chopped or snipped with scissors, instead of the raisins. It's worth adding the ginger and cumin if you have them but the cinnamon is the important one.

1 small <u>onion</u>, finely chopped

1 small <u>green pepper</u>, finely chopped

½ tsp <u>garlic</u> from a jar or tube

1½ mugs <u>minced lamb</u>

Large handful of <u>raisins</u>

¼ tsp <u>ground cinnamon</u>

¼ tsp <u>ground ginger</u> (optional)

¼ tsp <u>ground cumin</u> (optional)

¾ mug <u>boiling water</u>

1 <u>chicken stock cube</u>

2 tsp <u>clear honey</u>

2 tbsp <u>tomato purée</u>

<u>Salt and pepper</u>

¾ mug <u>couscous</u>

<u>Chopped fresh coriander</u>, optional to garnish

SERVE WITH

<u>Salad</u>

1 Put the onion, pepper, garlic and mince in a saucepan. Cook, stirring, until all the grains of meat are separate and no longer pink.

2 Stir in the raisins, spices, water, stock cube, honey, tomato purée and a little salt and pepper. Bring to the boil then turn down the heat to low and simmer for 20 minutes until rich and thick, stirring occasionally. Boil rapidly for a few minutes, stirring, if too thin.

3 Meanwhile, cook the couscous according to the packet directions. Fluff up with a fork.

4 Stir the lamb sauce. Taste and add more salt and pepper, if necessary.

5 Spoon the couscous on plates and spoon the sauce over. Scatter the coriander over, if using.

6 Serve with a salad.

Pork steps with **cabbage**

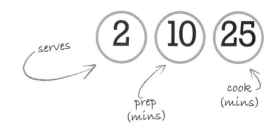

serves **2**

prep (mins) **10**

cook (mins) **25**

This is one of my favourite ways of serving pork steaks – it keeps them moist and succulent. If you don't have caraway seeds, add a pinch of dried basil instead. The rest of the cabbage will keep in the chiller to use on other days.

1 tbsp oil

2 pork shoulder steaks

1 small onion, thinly sliced

¼ tsp garlic from a jar or tube

¼ small cabbage, shredded

½ mug boiling water

½ vegetable stock cube

1 tbsp caraway seeds

Salt and pepper

2 potatoes, thinly sliced

Knob of butter or margarine

1 Heat the oil in a deep frying pan and fry the pork steaks for 2 minutes on each side to brown. Remove from the pan.

2 Add the onion, garlic and cabbage and fry for 2 minutes, stirring. Add the stock.

3 Lay the pork steaks on top, sprinkle with the caraway seeds and a little salt and pepper. Cover with the sliced potatoes and add small flakes of butter or margarine over the surface. Cover the pan with foil or a lid, reduce the heat and simmer for 20 minutes until tender. Serve straight from the pan.

Sweet & sour pork slices

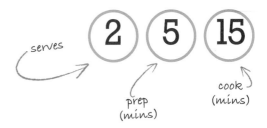

serves **2** prep (mins) **5** cook (mins) **15**

Belly pork is relatively cheap; choose lean rashers as some tend to be rather fatty. To make it stretch for three, add a drained can of bamboo shoots at step 3. Start cooking the rice in lightly salted water as soon as the pork is frying.

4 slices of <u>belly pork</u>
2 tsp <u>cornflour</u>
1 tbsp <u>vinegar</u>
250 g/1 small can <u>crushed</u>
<u>pineapple</u>
2 tbsp <u>tomato ketchup</u>
1 tbsp <u>soy sauce</u>
¼ <u>cucumber</u>, diced
1 large <u>carrot</u>, grated
SERVE WITH
<u>Plain boiled rice</u>

1 Discard any rind or bones from the pork and cut into chunks. Fry over a moderate heat for about 10 minutes, turning occasionally, until browned and cooked through. Remove from the pan.

2 Blend the cornflour with the vinegar.

3 Add the remaining ingredients to the pan and blend in the cornflour mixture. Bring to the boil, stirring. Return the pork to the pan and simmer for 3 minutes, stirring occasionally.

4 Serve with boiled rice.

Pork & noodle stir-fry

serves **2** prep (mins) **15** cook (mins) **10**

This is equally good with chicken, turkey or beef frying steak, diced or in strips. You could also omit the meat altogether and just add a drained can of bamboo shoots, a large handful of peas and sweetcorn and a sprinkling of peanuts.

1 slab Chinese egg noodles
2 slices of belly pork
1 tbsp oil
1 small onion, sliced
1 carrot, cut into matchsticks
1 small green pepper, cut into strips
4–6 mushrooms, sliced
¼ cucumber, cut into matchsticks
2 tbsp vinegar
2 tbsp soy sauce
1 tbsp sugar or honey
½ tsp ground ginger or Chinese five-spice powder
Salt and pepper

1 Cook the noodles according to the packet directions. Drain.

2 Using scissors, cut the rind and any bones off the pork and cut the meat into small pieces.

3 Heat the oil in a large pan or wok. Add the pork and fry for 4 minutes, stirring.

4 Add the vegetables and continue cooking, stirring, for 5 minutes.

5 Add the noodles and the remaining ingredients. Toss well until heated through. Taste and add a little more soy sauce, or sugar or honey, if liked. Serve straight away.

Sausage burgers with cheese

serves

4   5   10

prep (mins)   cook (mins)

Sausagemeat usually comes in 500 g packs so it's worth making up all four burgers and freezing the remainder to cook on other days. Alternatively, make only 2 burgers and use the rest for Toad in the hole (see page 137)

500 g pork sausagemeat

4 Mini Baby Bel cheeses, rind removed

OR

4 x 2.5 cm squares Cheddar or Edam cheese

1 tbsp oil

2 tbsp tomato relish or ketchup

4 burger buns

SERVE WITH

Salad

1 Shape the sausagemeat into 8 small flat cakes with wet hands (so it doesn't stick to them).

2 Place a Mini Baby Bel or square of cheese in the centre of each of the 4 cakes, then top with the remaining sausagemeat, pressing the edges well together to seal.

3 Either brush with the oil, then grill, or fry in the oil for 4–5 minutes on each side, turning once, until crisp, golden and cooked through. Drain on kitchen paper.

4 Spread the split buns with a little tomato relish or ketchup and add the burgers.

5 Serve with salad.

Sticky barbecue bangers & rice

serves **2** prep (mins) **5** cook (mins) **15**

This makes an interesting change from basic grilled or fried sausages. You can give pork shoulder steaks the same sticky glaze and they'll take a similar time to cook if you start them off in a tablespoon of oil.

½ mug long-grain rice
425 g/1 large can red kidney beans, drained
Salt and pepper
6 good-quality thick sausages
Knob of butter or margarine
1 tbsp vinegar
1 tbsp tomato purée
2 tsp brown sauce
1 tbsp golden syrup or honey

1 Cook the rice in plenty of boiling salted water for 10 minutes or according to packet directions, until just tender but still with some 'bite'. Drain in a colander and return to the pan.

2 Stir in the beans and a little salt and pepper. Cover and heat very gently, stirring until hot.

3 Meanwhile, fry the sausages in a large frying pan on a moderate heat with no extra fat, for about 10 minutes, turning occasionally until cooked through and browned all over. Remove from the pan.

4 Drain off the fat from the sausages, then stir in the butter or margarine until melted and blend in the remaining ingredients. Return the sausages to the pan and spoon the glaze over them. Cook for about 3 minutes until stickily coated.

5 Pile the rice mixture on to serving plates and top with the sausages. Serve hot.

Toad in the hole

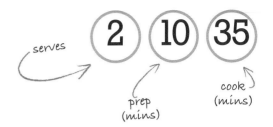

serves · 2 · 10 · 35
prep (mins)
cook (mins)

Add a handful of chopped onion or throw in a few diced peppers or sliced mushrooms when you cook the sausages if you like. If you use sausagemeat, use remainder for Sausage burgers with cheese (see page 135).

4-6 thick sausages, 6-8 chipolatas or ½ x 500 g block sausagemeat

2 tbsp oil

FOR THE BATTER

½ mug plain flour

Pinch of salt

1 egg

½ mug milk and water, mixed

½ tsp dried mixed herbs (optional)

SERVE WITH

Baked beans or canned tomatoes and a leafy green vegetable

1 Preheat the oven to 200°C/400°F/gas 6/fan oven 180°C.

2 Arrange the sausages, evenly spaced out in a smallish shallow baking tin or roll the sausagemeat into balls and put in the pan. Add the oil, then cook in the oven for 10 minutes until sizzling and starting to brown.

3 Put the flour and salt in a bowl. Add the egg and half the milk and water and gradually mix in, then whisk with a balloon whisk until smooth and bubbly. Stir in the remaining milk and water and add the herbs, if using.

4 Pour over the sausages and return to the oven for about 25 minutes until well risen, crisp and deep golden brown.

5 Serve hot with baked beans or canned tomatoes and a leafy green vegetable.

Sausage salar
with **croutons**

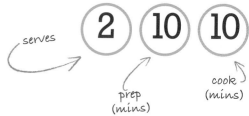

serves **2**

prep (mins) **10**

cook (mins) **10**

You get more sausages in a pack than you can eat on your own for one meal. Cook them all at the same time, then use the remainder cold for this salad. It's also a good way to use a few slices of bread that is past its best.

2 slices of <u>white bread</u>, cubed
2 tbsp <u>oil</u>
4 thick or 6–8 chipolata <u>sausages</u>, cooked and sliced
300 g/1 medium can <u>sweetcorn with peppers</u>, drained
425 g/1 large can <u>butter beans</u>, drained
¼ <u>cucumber</u>, diced
¼ tsp <u>garlic</u> from a jar or tube
4 tbsp <u>plain yoghurt</u>, <u>crème fraîche</u> or <u>mayonnaise</u>
1 tsp <u>dried chives</u> (optional)
<u>Salt and pepper</u>

1 Fry the cubes of bread in the hot oil until golden. Drain on kitchen paper.

2 Mix the sausages with the corn and peppers, butter beans and cucumber.

3 Mix the garlic purée with the yoghurt, crème fraîche or mayonnaise, the chives, if using, and a little salt and pepper.

4 Add the fried bread to the salad and toss. Pile on to serving plates and spoon the dressing on top.

Quick smoked sausage pilaf

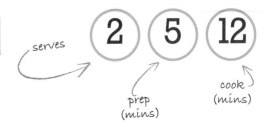

serves **2**

prep (mins) **5**

cook (mins) **12**

Smoked pork sausage will be near the frankfurters in the supermarket. Ring the changes by adding some diced peppers or mushrooms to the rice or substitute cooked ordinary sausages or diced ham for the smoked pork sausage.

½–¾ mug long-grain rice
1 mug frozen diced mixed vegetables
Knob of butter or margarine
1 onion, finely chopped
½ tsp chilli powder (optional)
½ tsp dried mixed herbs
1 x 225 g smoked pork sausage, sliced
Salt and pepper

1. Cook the rice in plenty of boiling lightly salted water for 10 minutes, or according to packet directions, until just tender. Add the vegetables after 5 minutes of cooking time. Drain, rinse with boiling water and drain again.

2. Meanwhile, melt the butter or margarine in a large frying pan. Add the onion and fry, stirring, for about 4 minutes until lightly golden.

3. Stir in the chilli powder, if using, the herbs and the sausage. Heat through for 2 minutes, stirring.

4. Add the rice and vegetable mixture, season to taste and cook, stirring, until piping hot.

Sauerkraut with frankfurters

serves **2** prep (mins) **3** cook (mins) **10**

Another option here is to thickly slice the hot potatoes and stir them into the sauerkraut. If you don't have caraway seeds, you can leave them out – it's not worth keeping too many spices in the cupboard.

1 Empty the sauerkraut into a pan, stir in the caraway seeds and heat through. Drain.

2 Meanwhile, heat the frankfurters according to the packet directions.

3 Serve with plain boiled potatoes and German or Dijon mustard.

200 g/1 small jar <u>sauerkraut</u>

1 tbsp <u>caraway seeds</u>

6–8 <u>frankfurters</u>

SERVE WITH

Plain boiled <u>potatoes</u> and <u>German</u> or <u>Dijon mustard</u>

Penne with ham **and peas**

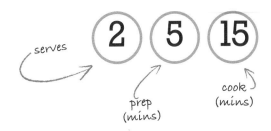

serves **2** prep (mins) **5** cook (mins) **15**

Cooked ham pieces are cheap on deli counters. They can look a bit of a mess but if you just take out any fatty bits and cut the rest into neat chunks, they're fine. You may also find enough good slices for sandwiches amongst them.

1 onion, finely chopped
¼ x 250 g tub butter or margarine
1 tbsp oil
2 handfuls of cooked ham pieces
Large handful of frozen peas
½ tsp dried mint (optional)
4 large handfuls penne or other pasta shapes
2 tbsp grated Parmesan-style cheese
Salt and pepper

1 Fry the onion gently in the butter or margarine and oil for a few minutes until soft but not brown.

2 Meanwhile, cut the ham into very small cubes, discarding any fat or gristle.

3 Add the ham and peas to the onions with the mint, if using. Cover, reduce the heat and cook gently for 5 minutes, stirring occasionally.

4 Cook the pasta according to the packet directions. Drain and return to the saucepan. Tip the ham mixture into the pasta and add the cheese. Toss well. Season to taste.

5 Pile on to warm plates and serve.

TIP For a creamier sauce, use half the butter or margarine and add a few spoonfuls of cream or crème fraîche before tossing.

Grilled ham with **pineapple**

serves → **2** **10** **15**

prep (mins)   cook (mins)

Packs of ham steaks are on the shelves with the bacon. They're much cheaper than gammon steaks. This is also a great way to cook with turkey steaks, but grill for a minute or two longer each side to make sure they're cooked through.

2 round <u>ham steaks</u>
200 g/1 small can <u>pineapple</u> <u>chunks</u>
2 <u>tomatoes</u>, chopped
2 slices of <u>cheese</u>
SERVE WITH
<u>Crusty bread</u> or <u>chips</u> and <u>green</u> <u>salad</u>

1 Snip the edges of the ham steaks with scissors to prevent curling.

2 Drain and roughly chop the pineapple and mix with the tomatoes.

3 Grill the ham for 3 minutes on each side.

4 Spread the pineapple mixture over the ham, and top with a slice of cheese.

5 Return to the grill until the cheese has melted and the fruit is hot.

6 Serve with crusty bread or chips and a green salad.

Cheese & ham pancakes

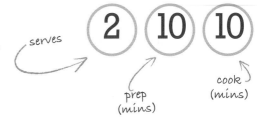

serves **2**

prep (mins) **10**

cook (mins) **10**

If eating alone, store the rest in foil and reheat quickly in a pan or microwave. Serve the pancakes for dessert, too, with butter, sugar and lemon juice, hot lemon sauce (see page 181) or smeared with chocolate spread then rolled up.

1 quantity <u>batter</u> (see Toad in the hole, page 137)
A little <u>oil</u> for frying
FOR THE FILLING
4 slices of <u>ham</u>
4 slices of <u>cheese</u> or 2 large handfuls of grated <u>Cheddar</u> <u>cheese</u>
2 <u>tomatoes</u>, sliced
SERVE WITH
<u>Salad</u>

1 Make the batter.

2 Pour a little oil in a non-stick frying pan. Swirl round, then pour off the excess. Heat until almost smoking. Add about a quarter of the batter, quickly swirl round the pan so it coats the base completely. Fry until bubbles appear and the top is set and looks dry. Flip over and cook the other side briefly.

3 Slide out of the pan on to a plate, cover with a lid and keep warm over a pan with a little gently simmering water in it. Heat a little more oil, pour off and repeat to cook the remaining pancakes.

4 Put a slice of ham and cheese (or a quarter of the grated cheese) and some slices of tomato on each one and fold over to form square parcels. Invert on serving plates. Serve straight away.

5 If you like the cheese really melted, flash briefly under a grill or pop each one in the microwave for a few seconds.

TIP Make sure the pan is really hot and oiled all over the base before you add the batter. Persevere if the first one isn't too perfect, the pan gets 'seasoned' as you cook and the remaining pancakes will cook much better!

Spaghetti
carbonara

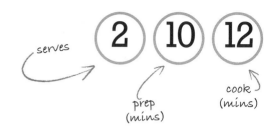

serves 2
prep (mins) 10
cook (mins) 12

Carbonara is a quick and easy dish and always popular. If you don't have bacon, chop up a pepperoni stick or a slice or two of ham and add them with the garlic at step 3.

⅓–½ x 500 g packet of spaghetti
1 small onion, chopped
2–3 bacon rashers, chopped
2 tbsp oil
½ tsp garlic from a jar or tube
Salt and pepper
1 tbsp chopped fresh parsley OR
½ tsp dried chives or mixed herbs
1 egg
1 tbsp milk
SERVE WITH
Grated Parmesan-style or
Cheddar cheese

1 Cook the spaghetti according to the packet directions. Drain and return to the pan.

2 Meanwhile, fry the onion and bacon in the oil for 1 minute.

3 Add the garlic, a little salt and pepper and the herbs. Cover with a lid and cook gently for 5 minutes until the onion is soft. Add to the pasta and toss well.

4 Beat the egg with the milk. Add to the pan and stir over a gentle heat until creamy but only just beginning to scramble. Don't overcook.

5 Spoon on to serving plates and top with lots of grated cheese.

Great British fry-up

 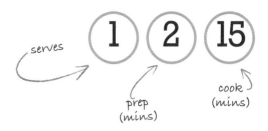
This is all about timing. Cook things in the right order and be patient – if the pan is too hot, it'll burn the outsides before the food is cooked through. You can double the quantities, but your pan is probably not large enough for more.

2 tbsp oil
1 sausage
1 hash brown
1 bacon rasher
1 slice of bread, cut in quarters
1 tomato, halved
200 g/½ large can baked beans
1 egg

1 Heat the oil slightly in a large frying pan, add the sausage and fry gently, turning regularly, for about 5 minutes until lightly browned.

2 Add the hash brown and bacon and fry for about 5 minutes until starting to brown, turning once. Keep turning the sausage occasionally.

3 Move everything to the sides of the pan to finish cooking on the lowest heat, add the bread and tomato to the centre and fry for about 2 minutes each side until golden.

4 Put the beans in the microwave or another pan to heat through.

5 Move everything to the side of the pan. Add a little more oil if the pan is dry. Break in the egg and turn the heat up slightly. Fry for 1–2 minutes, spooning the fat over the top until cooked how you like it.

6 Serve and enjoy straight away.

Simple cheese & bacon pasta

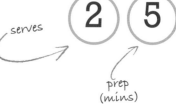

serves **2**

prep (mins) **5**

cook (mins) **12**

This is really easy, tasty and great when you haven't got loads in the cupboard. If you fancy a bit of crunch, add some grated carrots with the cheese. Or you can toss some carrots in a little oil and vinegar and serve them as a side salad.

Large handful of <u>bacon pieces</u> or
2–4 <u>bacon rashers</u>
4 large handfuls <u>pasta shapes</u>
1 mug grated <u>Red Leicester</u>,
<u>Cheddar</u> or <u>Edam cheese</u>
1 tsp <u>Worcestershire sauce</u>
<u>Salt and pepper</u>
Large knob of <u>butter</u> or
<u>margarine</u>

1 Remove any rind or bone from the bacon pieces, if using. Cut the bacon into small pieces. Fry with no extra fat until crisp, stirring all the time.

2 Meanwhile, cook the pasta according to the packet directions, drain and return to the pan.

3 Add the cheese, Worcestershire sauce, a little seasoning and the butter or margarine. Toss well until creamy.

4 Pile on to warm serving plates and serve sprinkled with the bacon.

Hot potato & bacon salad

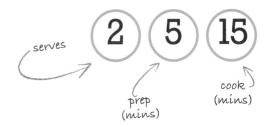

serves **2**

prep (mins) **5**

cook (mins) **15**

This is a delicious variation on a standard potato salad. If you don't have bacon, you can add some chopped ham, salami or similar when you mix the salad together. A good grinding of pepper spices up the flavour.

14 baby new potatoes, halved
Salt and pepper
2 streaky bacon rashers, rinded and chopped
2 tbsp boiling water
1 tbsp white wine vinegar
1 tbsp crème fraîche
1 spring onion, chopped
SERVE WITH
Salad

1 Cook the potatoes in boiling salted water for about 10 minutes until tender. Drain.

2 Heat the same pan to dry it, then fry the bacon until crisp and brown. Remove from the pan.

3 Add the boiling water and vinegar to the pan and bring back to the boil.

4 Remove from the heat and stir in the remaining ingredients. Season with salt and pepper.

5 Stir in the potatoes and bacon until well mixed.

6 Serve with salad.

Fish
meals

Brain food! Fish is incredibly good for you but can range from dirt cheap to staggeringly expensive. I've chosen the pick of the catch for high quality and low cost and have come up with some great ideas using canned fish, which is fantastically good value.

The good thing about fish is that any type can be cooked in any way, so don't be afraid to experiment. You'll find mackerel and herring are very good buys but white fish varies enormously in cost. Coley and pollack are often relatively cheap and farmed salmon is no longer the luxury it once was but always look out for special offers on the fresh fish counter.

Quick fish pot

serves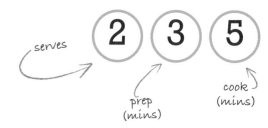

2 3 5

prep (mins)

cook (mins)

Coley is likely to be the cheapest fish you'll find, so it is ideal for this speedy stew. Because this recipe uses whole cans of vegetables as a throw-together meal, it will serve two very hungry people.

1 piece of fresh or frozen <u>white fish fillet</u>, about 175 g

400 g/1 large can <u>tomatoes</u>

½ mug <u>water</u>

1 <u>vegetable stock cube</u>

275 g/1 small can <u>new potatoes</u>, drained and quartered

275 g/1 small can <u>sliced carrots</u>, drained

275 g/1 small can <u>garden peas</u>, drained

<u>Salt and pepper</u>

¼ tsp <u>dried mixed herbs</u>

SERVE WITH

<u>Crusty bread</u>

1 Cut the fish into small chunks, discarding any skin and bones.

2 Place the tomatoes in a large saucepan and break up with a wooden spoon. Add the remaining ingredients, adding the fish last.

3 Bring to the boil, reduce the heat, cover and simmer for 5 minutes until the fish is tender. Stir gently and season to taste.

4 Ladle into large, warm soup bowls and serve with lots of crusty bread.

Thai fish curry

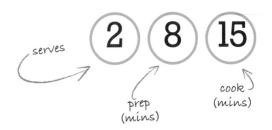

For two people, you only need half a can of coconut milk – store the rest in the fridge and use for Thai green chicken curry (see page 105) or make twice the quantity and reheat. To spice it up, sprinkle with dried chilli flakes to serve.

2 handfuls of fresh or frozen French beans
3½ mugs jasmine or long-grain rice
½ x 400 ml/1 large can coconut milk
1 tbsp Thai green curry paste
2 pollack or other white fish fillets, about 150 g each, cut into chunks, discarding skin
Salt and pepper

1   Trim off the tops and tails of the beans, if fresh, and cut into short lengths.

2   Boil in lightly salted water for 4–5 minutes until tender. Drain, reserving the water.

3   Put the water back in the pan with a little more boiling water. Add a little more salt. Bring back to the boil, add the rice, stir well and boil for 10 minutes or until just tender. Drain.

4   While the rice is cooking, mix the coconut milk and curry paste in a separate saucepan, add the fish. Season lightly. Bring to the boil, reduce the heat, cover and simmer for 5 minutes until the fish is cooked.

5   Stir in the beans. Taste and re-season if necessary.

6   Spoon the rice into bowls and spoon the curry over.

Mustard
mackerel

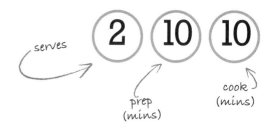

serves **2** prep (mins) **10** cook (mins) **10**

Mackerel is excellent value and really nutritious. If you buy from a fish counter, ask the assistant to cut off the heads and gut them for you. If pre-packed, they will already be cleaned.

2 whole <u>mackerel</u>, cleaned
<u>Salt and pepper</u>
2 large knobs of <u>butter</u> or <u>margarine</u>
2 tsp <u>oil</u>
1 tsp <u>mustard</u>
¼ tsp <u>sugar</u>
½ tsp <u>vinegar</u> or <u>lemon juice</u>
<u>Salt and pepper</u>
SERVE WITH
<u>Potatoes</u> and <u>broad beans</u>, <u>peas</u> or <u>spinach</u>

1 Cut the heads off the mackerel if you prefer, and wipe inside and out with kitchen paper. Make 3 or 4 diagonal slashes across each side of the fish with a sharp knife and season with salt and pepper.

2 Heat a large knob of the butter or margarine with the oil in a large frying pan.

3 Add the fish and fry for about 5 minutes on each side until browned and cooked through. (You can serve the fish plain just like this if you wish.)

4 Remove the fish from the pan and transfer to warm serving plates.

5 Add the remaining butter or margarine to the pan juices with the mustard, sugar, vinegar or lemon juice, and a little salt and pepper. Stir until melted and bubbling.

6 Pour over the fish. Serve with potatoes and broad beans, peas or spinach.

Egg foo yung with rice

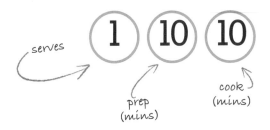

serves 1 10 10

prep (mins)

cook (mins)

Crab sticks are inexpensive and tasty (albeit they've never seen a crab in their lives!). You can substitute prawns if you are feeling flash or they're on special offer. You could make double the quantity and eat the other cold the next day.

¼ mug long-grain rice

Salt

2 eggs

1 tsp soy sauce, plus extra for serving

Pepper

2 spring onions or a small onion, finely chopped

Handful of frozen peas, thawed

4 crab sticks, thawed if frozen and cut in chunks

Pinch of Chinese five-spice powder

1 tbsp sunflower oil

1 Bring a smallish saucepan of water to the boil. Add a pinch of salt and the rice. Bring back to the boil and boil for 10 minutes, or according to packet directions, until the rice is cooked and tender, but still has some 'bite'. Drain in a colander.

2 Meanwhile, using a fork or metal whisk, mix the eggs in a bowl with the soy sauce and a little pepper. Stir in the spring onions, peas, crab sticks and spice.

3 Heat the oil in a frying pan over a moderate heat. Add the egg mixture and cook, lifting and stirring the mixture until golden brown underneath and almost set.

4 Turn the egg over with a fish slice or tip it out on to a plate, so the browned side is up and slide it back into the pan, and cook the other side briefly.

5 Fold in three and slide on to a warm serving plate with the rice. Sprinkle with soy sauce and serve.

Fish in tomato & pepper sauce

serves **2** prep (mins) **10** cook (mins) **15**

Cod is the classic for this Provençal-style dish but any fish will do – try coley or, even, farmed salmon, which is very inexpensive. Olives aren't cheap but they keep for ages in the fridge and even a couple add flavour and texture.

1 tbsp oil
1 green pepper, thinly sliced
½ tsp garlic from a jar or tube
400 g/1 large can tomatoes
1 tbsp tomato purée
Large pinch of sugar
225 g white fish fillet, skinned and cubed
Salt and pepper
A few stoned olives, halved (optional)
SERVE WITH
Plain boiled rice and mixed salad or green beans

1 Heat the oil in a saucepan, add the pepper and fry gently over a moderate heat, stirring, for 3 minutes to soften but not brown.

2 Add the garlic and tomatoes and break up with a wooden spoon. Add the tomato purée and sugar, bring to the boil and boil rapidly for 5 minutes, stirring occasionally until pulpy.

3 Add the fish, turn down the heat and cook gently for 3–5 minutes until the fish is cooked but not breaking up.

4 Season to taste and serve on a bed of boiled rice, with a mixed salad or green beans.

Fish & potato fry

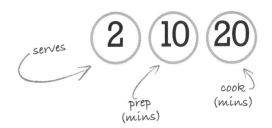

serves

2 10 20

prep (mins) cook (mins)

There's no need to peel the potatoes first – the skin is good for you and lots of nutrients lie just under it (it also saves time and effort). If you like onion, grate half a small one with the potatoes.

1 tbsp oil
2 large potatoes, grated
2 small fish fillets, any kind, skinned and cubed
Salt and pepper
400 g/1 large can tomatoes
SERVE WITH
Peas

1 Heat the oil in a frying pan. Add half the grated potatoes and press down well. Season.

2 Add the fish in a layer, then top with the remaining potatoes, press down and season again.

3 Cover with a lid or foil and cook over a gentle heat for about 20 minutes until cooked through. To test, push a knife down through, there should be no resistance. Don't cook on a high heat or it will burn before it cooks through.

4 Meanwhile, heat the tomatoes in a saucepan with a little pepper.

5 Loosen the fish and potato fry with a fish slice and turn out on to a warmed serving plate, browned side up.

6 Cut in half and serve with the tomatoes and peas.

Tuna salad with garlic & cheese

serves **2** prep (mins) **10** cook (mins) **6**

You could make this go round for more people by adding a couple of hard-boiled eggs cut in chunks or perhaps a drained can of sweetcorn or haricot beans.

Handful of fresh or frozen green beans, cut in short lengths
3 tbsp oil
4 slices of French bread, or 1 thick slice from a large loaf, cubed
½ x 200 g small carton soft cheese with garlic and herbs
3 tbsp milk
2 tsp vinegar or lemon juice
¼ small crisp lettuce
200 g/1 small can tuna, drained and flaked
2 tomatoes, cut into wedges

1 Boil the beans in lightly salted water for 3–4 minutes until just tender but still with a little bite. Drain, rinse with cold water and drain again.

2 Heat 2 of the tablespoons of oil and fry the bread cubes until golden on each side. Drain well on kitchen paper.

3 Whisk the cheese in a large bowl with the milk, oil and vinegar or lemon juice until smooth.

4 Tear the lettuce into neat pieces. Add to the bowl.

5 Add the beans, tuna and bread cubes and toss gently. Divide into two serving bowls and garnish with tomato wedges.

Tuna mornay

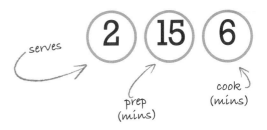

serves 2
prep (mins) 15
cook (mins) 6

You can make this with canned pink salmon for a change and serve it with toast instead of crusty bread. You could also serve it with rice, to make a more substantial meal. It will reheat well in the microwave.

2 large knobs of <u>butter</u> or <u>margarine</u>
2 <u>onions</u>, thinly sliced
3 tbsp <u>plain flour</u>
1 mug <u>milk</u>
<u>Salt and pepper</u>
Large handful of grated <u>Cheddar cheese</u>
200 g/1 small can <u>tuna</u>, drained
SERVE WITH
<u>Crusty bread</u> and a <u>salad</u>

1 Melt the butter or margarine in a saucepan. Add the onions and cook, stirring, over a fairly high heat, for 3 minutes until softened and lightly golden.

2 Stir the flour into the pan and cook for 1 minute. Remove from the heat and gradually stir in the milk, seasoning and half the cheese. Return to the heat, bring to the boil and cook for 2 minutes, stirring.

3 Preheat the grill.

4 Tip the tuna into a flameproof dish and break up with a fork. Pour the sauce over and sprinkle with the remaining cheese.

5 Cook under the grill for about 6 minutes until golden, bubbling and hot through. Serve with crusty bread and a salad.

One-pot kedgeree

serves

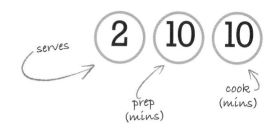

2   10   10

prep (mins)   cook (mins)

You can use ready-cooked smoked mackerel instead of the yellow fish, cut in pieces and added at step 4 to heat through. Or use smoked salmon trimmings. Store any remainder covered in the fridge and eat hot or cold the following day.

2 eggs, scrubbed under the cold tap
½–1 mug long-grain rice
Large pinch of salt
1 piece of yellow smoked fish fillet, about 125 g
½ mug frozen peas
A splash of milk
Pepper
Grated nutmeg (optional)
Small handful of chopped fresh parsley (optional)

1. Put the eggs in a large pan of water and bring to the boil. Add the rice and salt. Bring back to the boil and boil for 5 minutes.

2. Add the fish and peas and cook for a further 5 minutes.

3. Remove the fish and eggs. Put the eggs in cold water. Drain the rice and peas and return to the saucepan.

4. Break up the fish, discard the skin and any bones. Shell the eggs and roughly cut up.

5. Add the fish and eggs to the rice and peas with the milk, salt and pepper and the nutmeg and/or parsley, if using. Heat through, stirring gently. Serve hot, straight from the dish.

Tuna, cheese & sweetcorn

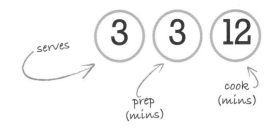

serves 3

prep (mins) 3

cook (mins) 12

This makes a small can of tuna and sweetcorn go a long way! If you need to reheat it, add a little milk to thin it a bit and stir well in a saucepan so it doesn't stick. Alternatively, reheat in the microwave, stirring occasionally.

½ x 500 g packet of pasta shapes
1 quantity of cheese sauce (see Macaroni cheese, page 67)
200 g/1 small can tuna, drained
200 g/1 small can sweetcorn, drained
SERVE WITH
Cheddar cheese, grated (optional) and a green salad

1   Cook the pasta according to the packet directions, then drain.

2   Meanwhile, make the cheese sauce. Add the drained tuna and sweetcorn, stir and heat through.

3   Add the drained pasta and toss together well. Spoon on to plates.

4   Serve topped with a little grated cheese, if liked, and salad.

Salmon
macaroni

serves 2 5 10

prep (mins)

cook (mins)

Cans of pink salmon are not too expensive and are a great standby to keep in the cupboard. You don't need much to make a tasty pasta dish, and you can always add more vegetables – a handful of frozen peas works well.

4 large handfuls of <u>macaroni</u>
<u>Salt and pepper</u>
4 tbsp <u>plain flour</u>
1 mug <u>milk</u>
2 tbsp <u>butter</u> or <u>margarine</u>
200 g/1 small can <u>pink salmon</u>
2 tbsp <u>tomato ketchup</u>
2 handfuls of <u>Cheddar cheese</u>

1 Cook the macaroni in boiling salted water according to the packet directions.

2 While it is cooking, whisk the flour and milk in a pan, then add the butter or margarine and bring to the boil, whisking all the time.

3 Add the salmon and its juices, the ketchup, salt and pepper and stir in.

4 Drain the macaroni, then stir it into the sauce.

5 Serve sprinkled with cheese.

Salmon & potato **salad**

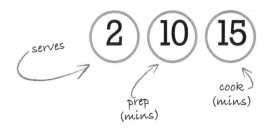

serves **2** prep (mins) **10** cook (mins) **15**

Here's something for when you want a dish that's a little bit special. You can buy salmon steaks individually wrapped or in frozen packs, often very reasonably priced.

10 small <u>new potatoes</u>
<u>Salt and pepper</u>
2 <u>salmon steaks</u>
2 handfuls <u>lettuce leaves</u>, torn in pieces
2 <u>tomatoes</u>, cut into wedges
small piece of <u>cucumber</u>, cut into chunks
1 small <u>onion</u>, chopped
2 tbsp <u>olive oil</u>
2 tsp <u>lemon juice</u> or <u>vinegar</u>
1 tsp <u>Worcestershire sauce</u>
Pinch of <u>sugar</u>
2 tbsp <u>mayonnaise</u>

1 Cook the potatoes in boiling salted water for about 10 minutes until tender, then drain.

2 Meanwhile, grill the salmon on foil for about 10 minutes until cooked through.

3 Mix the salad ingredients in a bowl.

4 Whisk the oil, lemon juice, Worcestershire sauce and sugar. Pour over the salad and toss together.

5 Arrange the salad on plates with the potatoes to the side. Top with the salmon and finish with a spoonful of mayonnaise.

Fish creole

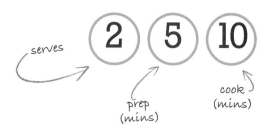

serves **2** **5** **10**

prep (mins)

cook (mins)

If you prefer a less spicy taste, use paprika or even garam masala or curry powder instead of chilli powder. It's even better with strips of streaky bacon wrapped round the fish before frying.

½ mug long grain rice
2 white fish fillets, about 150 g each, with skin on
1 tbsp plain flour
Salt and pepper
¼ tsp chilli powder
Large knob of butter or margarine
1 tbsp oil
1 banana, cut into chunks
A few lime or lemon wedges (optional)
SERVE WITH
Plain boiled rice and a green salad

1. Cook the rice in boiling, lightly salted water for 10 minutes or according to the packet directions. Drain in a colander.

2. Meanwhile, dust the fish with flour mixed with a little salt and pepper and the chilli powder.

3. Heat half the butter or margarine and the oil in a frying pan and fry the fish for 3 minutes on each side until lightly golden and cooked through.

4. Transfer to a warm serving dish and keep warm.

5. Add the remaining butter or margarine and oil to the pan and stir-fry the banana for about 2 minutes until softening. Transfer to the serving dish.

6. Garnish with lime or lemon wedges, if liked, and serve hot with rice and a green salad.

Prawn risotto

serves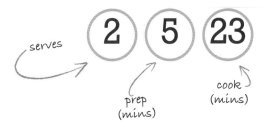

2 5 23

prep (mins)

cook (mins)

Look out for prawns on special offer for a quick cooking and tasty treat, or substitute chunks of crab stick. For another delicious option, use half milk and half stock, and chunks of smoked haddock.

1 vegetable or fish stock cube
1½ mugs boiling water
Knob of butter or margarine
1 small onion, finely chopped
½ mug risotto rice
1 mug prawns
2 tbsp soft white cheese OR double cream
Salt and pepper

1 Dissolve the stock cube in a mug of the boiling water.

2 Melt the butter or margarine in a saucepan. Add the onion and fry, stirring, for 3 minutes until the onion is soft.

3 Stir in the rice until glistening.

4 Stir in a little of the hot stock and water, and simmer, stirring, until the rice has absorbed the water.

5 Keep gradually adding the stock in this way until it has all been absorbed and the rice is just tender and slightly creamy. This will take 15–20 minutes.

6 Stir in the prawns and soft white cheese or cream, season to taste and heat through. Serve immediately.

almost finished

Extra energy fodder

Get yourself geared up to make a batch of any of the following before you have to get stuck into revising or serious exam schedules. Then you'll have something highly comforting and packed with a great energy boost for when your spirits are flagging or you simply haven't got time to stop for a proper meal (like breakfast when you've overslept from all that study ... or whatever!). None of them takes long to make and they are all far cheaper than buying equivalent bars in the supermarket or health food shop.

Peanut honey bites

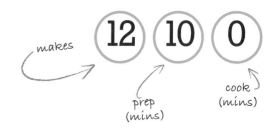

makes **12**
prep (mins) **10**
cook (mins) **0**

These biscuits make a nutritious snack when serious study is at hand. Look out for packets of broken biscuits or own-brands, they're really inexpensive and ideal for this recipe.

½ x 250 g tub <u>butter</u> or <u>hard</u> <u>margarine</u>
3 tbsp <u>thick honey</u>
⅔ x 300 g packet of <u>plain</u> <u>biscuits</u>, roughly crushed
1 tsp grated <u>lemon rind</u> (optional)
3 tbsp <u>crunchy peanut butter</u>

1 Melt the butter or margarine with the honey and bring to the boil. Remove from the heat.

2 Stir in the remaining ingredients and mix well.

3 Press into a greased 18 cm square baking tin or similar sized container and chill until set. Cut into squares and store in an airtight tin.

Chewy fruit & **coconut bars**

makes **15** **10** **0**

prep (mins)   cook (mins)

These bars are great energy boosters during cramming sessions. You can substitute any other dried fruit – such as dates, prunes or raisins – for the apricots if you prefer.

175 g/1 small can evaporated milk
4 tsp thick honey
3 tbsp apple or orange juice
¼ x 250 g tub butter or margarine
¼ mug light brown (preferably) sugar
2 large handfuls of sultanas
1 mug ready-to-eat dried apricots, chopped or snipped with scissors
½ mug desiccated coconut
2 mugs rolled oats

1 Heat the evaporated milk with the honey, juice, butter or margarine and sugar until just melted. Remove from the heat.

2 Add the remaining ingredients and mix well. Press into a greased 28 x 18 cm baking tin or similar sized container.

3 Wrap in clingfilm or put in a clean plastic carrier bag and chill overnight to set and allow the flavours to develop before cutting into bars.

4 Store in an airtight container in the fridge.

Cinnamon
french toast

This has to be comfort food at its best! To turn this old favourite into a really nutritious snack, you could cut an apple into wedges or a banana into chunks to eat with the toast.

1 egg
2 tbsp milk
4 thick slices of bread, crusts removed
Large knob of butter or margarine
2 tbsp oil
1 tbsp caster sugar, heaped
1 tsp cinnamon

1 Beat the egg and milk together. Dip the bread in to coat it completely, allowing it to soak in well.

2 Heat the butter or margarine and oil in a large frying pan. Fry the slices for about $1\frac{1}{2}$ minutes over a high heat until a deep golden brown, turning once.

3 Drain on kitchen paper.

4 Mix the sugar and cinnamon on a flat plate or put in a plastic bag. Dip the bread into the mixture until coated on both sides or drop into the bag hold the top together and shake it firmly. Serve straight away cut into triangles.

No-bake crunch bars

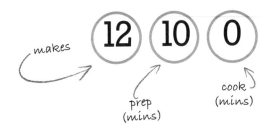

makes **12** **10** **0**

prep (mins)   cook (mins)

Chocolate is comfort food at its best. If you buy a good quality one with high cocoa solids, it's actually good for you (in small portions) as it is high in antioxidants and stimulates endorphins in your brain to make you feel good.

⅔ x 250 g tub <u>butter</u> or <u>margarine</u>
¼ mug <u>light brown</u> (preferably) <u>sugar</u>
2 tbsp <u>golden syrup</u>
3 tbsp <u>cocoa powder</u>
½ mug <u>raisins</u>
3 mugs <u>oat crunch-type cereal</u>
200 g bar <u>plain chocolate</u>

1 Oil and line the base of an 18 x 28 cm baking tin, or similar sized container, with baking parchment, greaseproof paper or the inside wrapper from a cereal packet.

2 Melt the butter or margarine, sugar and syrup and cocoa in a large saucepan. Remove from the heat. Stir in the raisins and cereal until well blended. Press into the tin.

3 Melt the chocolate in a pan over hot water and spread over the top, right into the corners.

4 Chill until set, cut into fingers and store in an airtight tin.

Mum's
flapjacks

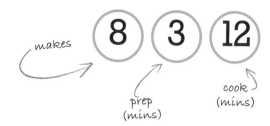

makes **8** prep (mins) **3** cook (mins) **12**

Easy and delicious – and, of course, oats are good for you. When you want a real taste of home, you can't beat a good flapjack. Plus they transport well so you can take one with you for a mid-morning snack.

⅓ x 250 g tub <u>butter</u> or <u>margarine</u>
2 tbsp <u>brown sugar</u>
2 tbsp <u>golden syrup</u>
1½ mugs <u>porridge oats</u>
⅓ mug <u>plain flour</u>

1 Preheat the oven to 190°C/375°F/gas 5/fan oven 170°C and grease an 18 cm square baking tin.

2 Melt the butter, sugar and syrup in a pan.

3 Stir in the remaining ingredients and mix well.

4 Cook in the oven for about 12 minutes until golden.

5 Leave to cool for 5 minutes, then mark into portions. Leave to cool completely before removing from the tin.

6 Store in an airtight container.

Banana sultana flapjacks

makes **16** prep (mins) **8** cook (mins) **30**

This recipe was hailed by a medical student friend of mine and her flat mates as the food they lived on most! It's cheap, nutritious and delicious when you're studying – or when you're just chilling.

⅓ x 250 g tub <u>butter</u> or <u>margarine</u>, softened
½ mug <u>light brown</u> (preferably) <u>sugar</u>
1 tbsp <u>golden syrup</u> or <u>honey</u>
1 large, ripe <u>banana</u>, mashed
2 handfuls of <u>sultanas</u> or <u>raisins</u>
2½ mugs <u>porridge oats</u>

1 Preheat the oven to 180°C/350°F/gas 4/fan oven 160°C.

2 Put the butter or margarine, sugar and syrup or honey in a bowl and beat with a wooden spoon until smooth and fluffy.

3 Stir in the remaining ingredients and press into a greased 18 x 28 cm baking tin.

4 Bake in the oven for about 30 minutes or until golden brown.

5 Leave to cool for 10 minutes then mark into fingers with the back of a knife. Leave until completely cold before cutting up. Store in an airtight tin.

Simple
desserts

If you're health conscious, you'll live off yoghurts or fresh fruit for 'afters', which is a great idea and it's economical. But every now and then you might hanker after a real pudding – a bit of comfort food once again. Here are some dead easy ideas which taste terrific and are ideal for filling up on – especially when you have some friends around for a meal.

Ice cream & chocolate sauces

serves 4
prep (mins) 5
cook (mins) 5

Ice cream is a great standby. You can buy all kinds of fruit or toffee sauces, sprinkle on some nuts, chopped fruit or drizzle with honey – but nothing beats a chocolate or caramel option, so here are two to try.

8 scoops of ice cream
FOR THE CARAMEL SAUCE
2 Mars bars, chopped
4 tbsp milk
knob of butter or margarine
FOR THE CHOCOLATE SAUCE
1 x 200 g bar plain chocolate, broken into pieces
4 tbsp butter or margarine
3 tbsp brown or caster sugar
2 tbsp golden syrup
¾ mug milk

1 To make the caramel sauce, melt the Mars bars, milk and butter or margarine gently in a pan, stirring occasionally until melted. Add a little more milk if too thick.

2 To make the chocolate sauce, set a heatproof bowl on top of a pan of gently simmering water. Add the chocolate and butter or margarine and stir until completely melted.

3 Add the sugar and syrup, stirring until dissolved.

4 Slowly pour in the milk and stir gently until the mixture thickens.

5 To serve, pour the hot sauce over the ice cream in bowls and serve straight away.

Banana rice pudding layer

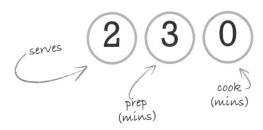

serves **2**

prep (mins) **3**

cook (mins) **0**

If making this for one person, save the rest of the rice pudding in a covered container in the fridge. Eat it the following day, with a handful of raisins and a pinch of cinnamon mixed in. If you prefer, heat the rice before layering.

1 Toss the bananas in the lemon juice.

2 Put a quarter of the bananas in each of two glasses. Top each with a quarter of the rice. Add the remaining bananas, then rice.

3 Add a spoonful of jam to the top of each.

2 bananas, sliced
1 tsp bottled lemon juice
410 g/1 large can creamed rice pudding
2 tsp strawberry or raspberry jam

Rhubarb & custard **charlotte**

serves **4** prep (mins) **10** cook (mins) **40**

If you've got four apples that need eating up, use them instead of the rhubarb. Peel and quarter them, cut out the cores and then slice them and add a squeeze of lemon juice and a sprinkling of sugar.

Large knob of <u>butter</u> or <u>margarine</u>, melted
4 slices of <u>bread</u>
1 individual carton <u>custard</u>
550 g/1 large can <u>rhubarb</u>, drained, reserving the juice
1 tbsp <u>light brown sugar</u>

1 Preheat the oven to 200°C/400°F/gas 6/fan oven 180°C and grease an ovenproof dish with half the melted butter or margarine.

2 Line the dish with 2½ slices of the bread.

3 Spread the custard in the base, then top with the drained fruit.

4 Dice the remaining bread, toss in the remaining melted butter or margarine and sugar and spoon over the top.

5 Bake in the oven for about 40 minutes until golden. Serve with the reserved juice.

Pineapple pudding

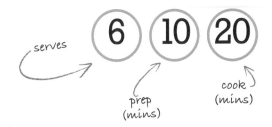

serves **6**
prep (mins) **10**
cook (mins) **20**

This pudding is just as good cold as hot. You can use canned peaches instead of pineapple or try pears and use a chocolate sponge cake mix. It's great to keep in the fridge to cut-and-come-again to over a few days.

Knob of butter or margarine
2 tbsp light brown sugar or golden syrup
225 g/1 small can pineapple rings, drained, reserving the juice
Glacé cherries, halved or a few sultanas
1 packet sponge cake mix
Egg and water according to the packet directions

1 Preheat the oven to 190°C/375°F/gas 5/fan oven 170°C and liberally grease a 20 cm round sandwich tin or a shallow ovenproof dish with the butter or margarine.

2 Sprinkle the sugar over the base, then top with the pineapple rings.

3 Place a halved glacé cherry, cut-side up, in the centre of each ring, or a few sultanas or raisins here and in the gaps around.

4 Make up the sponge mixture according to the packet directions. Spoon over the fruit.

5 Bake in the oven for 20 minutes until risen and the centre springs back when lightly pressed.

6 Leave to cool slightly in the tin, then loosen the edges with a round bladed knife and turn out on to a serving plate. Serve with the juice.

Almost instant chocolate **mousse**

serves **4** prep (mins) **5** cook (mins) **0**

This is so easy but tastes fantastic. The only effort is whipping the cream with a hand whisk if you don't have an electric one. For a special occasion, add a tablespoon of spirits such as vodka, rum or whisky with the chocolate.

300 ml/1 medium carton
double or whipping cream
2 heaped tbsp chocolate spread
(or chocolate and hazelnut)
A little chocolate, grated
(optional)

1 Whip the cream in a large bowl with a metal whisk until it stands in soft peaks. Spoon off about a third and reserve.

2 Add the chocolate spread to the remainder and whisk gently until thoroughly combined. Spoon into glasses or dishes and top with the reserved cream. If liked, grate a little chocolate over the surface to decorate.

3 Chill for 1–2 hours to firm up a bit.

Lemon pie

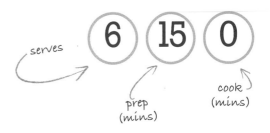

serves **6** — prep (mins) **15** — cook (mins) **0**

Serve this plain or top it with some grated chocolate or desiccated coconut. First toast the coconut in a dry frying pan, stirring until golden, then tip it out straight away and cool before putting on the pie. Store leftovers in the fridge.

225 g packet coconut ring biscuits
½ x 250 g tub butter or margarine, melted
300 ml/1 medium carton double or whipping cream
350 g/1 medium can sweetened condensed milk
8 tbsp bottled lemon juice

1 Put the biscuits in a plastic bag and crush finely with a bottle or rolling pin. Mix with the melted butter or margarine.

2 Press into the base of a large flan dish or other shallow, round dish.

3 Lightly whip the cream with a metal whisk until it's standing in soft peaks then gently whisk in the condensed milk and lemon juice.

4 When thickening, tip on to the biscuit base and level the surface. Chill overnight to set.

Caramel apples

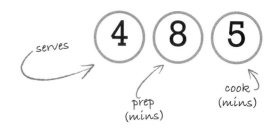

serves **4**
prep (mins) **8**
cook (mins) **5**

This is a great way of using up last week's apples that are looking a little 'tired'. I recommend peeling them before slicing as the skins are likely to be tough. You can give unripe pears the same treatment.

½ x 250 g tub <u>butter</u> or <u>margarine</u>
4 <u>eating apples</u>, quartered, cored and sliced
4 tbsp <u>light brown sugar</u>
½ tsp <u>mixed spice</u> or <u>cinnamon</u>
Handful of <u>sultanas</u>
SERVE WITH
<u>Whipped cream</u> or <u>yoghurt</u>

1 Melt the butter or margarine in a frying pan.

2 Add the apples and sprinkle with the sugar. Fry, tossing occasionally, for about 3 minutes until the sugar has melted.

3 Add the mixed spice and the sultanas and toss gently together.

4 Serve with whipped cream or yoghurt.

Bananas & hot lemon sauce

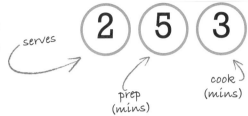

serves **2**

prep (mins) **5**

cook (mins) **3**

This hot lemon sauce is great just spooned over ice cream or with pancakes (see page 143). You could serve it more like a banana split with the banana halved lengthways, scoops of ice cream in the middle and the sauce spooned over.

Large knob of <u>butter</u> or <u>margarine</u>

3 tbsp <u>light brown sugar</u> or <u>honey</u>

1 tbsp <u>lemon juice</u>

1 small carton <u>plain yoghurt</u> OR 4 spoonfuls <u>ice cream</u>

2 <u>bananas</u>, sliced

1 Put the margarine, sugar and lemon juice in a small pan. Heat gently, stirring until well blended and the sugar has melted, if using. Simmer for 1 minute.

2 Divide the yoghurt or ice cream between 2 glasses. Top with sliced bananas.

3 Spoon the sauce over and serve straight away.

Banana split & chocolate sauce

serves **2**

prep (mins) **5**

cook (mins) **0**

This old favourite is so quick and easy to make – with the added bonus that you have here the quickest chocolate sauce that you can create in minutes to pour over just about anything. The ultimate comfort food.

2 bananas, split lengthways
4 scoops vanilla ice cream
2 large spoonfuls chocolate spread
A little milk or water
A few chopped nuts (optional)

1 Put the bananas and ice cream in serving dishes.

2 Put the chocolate spread in a pan and add a splash of milk or water. Heat gently, stirring all the time until smooth and runny. Add a little more milk or water, if necessary, to give a pouring consistency.

3 Pour over the bananas and ice cream and serve sprinkled with a few chopped nuts, if you like.

No-effort
fruit crumble

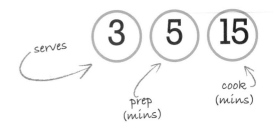

serves **3**

prep (mins) **5**

cook (mins) **15**

This is a really nutritious dessert, great to put in the oven when you're using it for a main course anyway. You can, of course, use any canned fruit you like – rhubarb is good, but so are apples, peaches or apricots.

410 g/1 large can <u>fruit</u>, drained, reserving the juice

¼ x 250 g tub <u>butter</u> or <u>margarine</u>

2 <u>Weetabix</u>

1 tbsp <u>light brown</u> (preferably) <u>sugar</u>

½ tsp <u>ground ginger</u>, <u>cinnamon</u> or <u>mixed spice</u>

SERVE WITH

<u>Cream</u> or <u>custard</u>

1 Preheat the oven to 190°C/375°F/gas 5/fan oven 170°C.

2 Put the fruit in an ovenproof dish.

3 Melt the butter or margarine in a saucepan.

4 Remove from the heat and crumble in the Weetabix. Stir in the sugar and spice.

5 Sprinkle the topping over the fruit, pressing down lightly.

6 Bake in the oven for about 15 minutes until crisp. Serve warm with cream or custard.

Banoffee
brûlée

 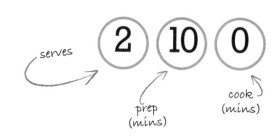
You could make other brûlées the same way using different fruits in season, such as sliced strawberries, plums or nectarines with the matching fruit yoghurt or vanilla yoghurt and the sugar over the top.

2 bananas
1 small carton toffee yoghurt
2-3 tbsp light brown sugar

1 Preheat the grill.

2 Slice the bananas and place in 2 individual flameproof dishes.

3 Spoon the yoghurt over.

4 Sprinkle liberally with the sugar to cover the tops completely.

5 Remove the grill rack and place the dishes in the pan. Grill until the sugar melts and bubbles.

6 Serve straight away or leave to cool, then chill before serving.

Easy strawberry cheesecake

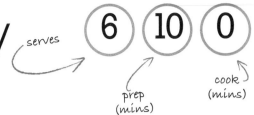

serves **6** prep (mins) **10** cook (mins) **0**

This is great if you're having a party. As with other desserts the only effort is whipping the cream but – particularly if you use double rather than the thinner whipping type – it doesn't take long.

23 cm <u>sponge flan case</u>
200 g carton <u>white soft cheese</u>
4 tbsp <u>caster sugar</u>
½ tsp <u>vanilla essence</u>
1 small carton <u>double cream</u>
400 g/1 large can <u>strawberry pie filling</u>

1 Put the flan case on a serving plate.

2 Mix the cheese with the sugar and vanilla essence in a bowl until well blended, using a wooden spoon.

3 Pour the cream into a separate bowl and whip with a metal whisk until softly peaking. Gently stir it into the cheese mixture. Spoon into the flan case, spread out and chill until fairly firm.

4 Spread the strawberry pie filling over the top before serving.

Index

apples, caramel 180

bacon
    bacon butty 34
    great British fry-up 145
    hot potato and bacon salad 147
    simple cheese and bacon pasta 146
    spaghetti carbonara 144
bananas
    banana rice pudding layer 175
    banana split and chocolate sauce 182
    bananas and hot lemon sauce 181
    banoffee brûlée 184
barbecue bangers and rice, sticky 136
basics
    making 15–16
    shopping 13–14
beans
    bean stew with dumplings 79
    black bean vegetable stir-fry 89
    curried bean and rice salad 88
    double tomato and bean soup 62
    great British fry-up 145
    omelette with green beans 45
    quick bean bake 80
beating, defined 19
beef
    beef hot pot 120
    chilli con carne 117
    chilli tacos in minutes 126
    home-made burgers 112
    lasagne al forno 116
    meat loaf 113
    piquant pan-fried steak 123
    potato moussaka 122
    quick beef pasta 114

    rich mince with new potatoes 118
    spaghetti bolognese 115
    see also corned beef
boiling
    eggs 15
    green vegetables 17
    potatoes 15–16
    rice 17
    root vegetables 17
bread
    bacon butty 34
    cheese and onion sandwich 43
    chicken and pesto baguette 56
    croque monsieur 42
    fish finger and mayonnaise (roll) 31
    herb and salami garlic bread 51
    mushroom omelette baguette 41
    stuffed naan bread wedges 37
    see also pitta bread; toast
breakfast, great British fry-up 145
broccoli with ham and cheese 128
burgers
    home-made burgers 112
    sausage burgers with cheese 135

cabbage, pork steaks with 132
cans, basics checklist 14
caramel apples 180
carbohydrates 9
carrots
    cooking techniques 17
    peppered liver with carrot mash 124
cheese
    broccoli with ham and cheese 128
    cheese and ham pancakes 143
    cheese and mushroom wedges 75

cheese and onion pitta bread 49
cheese and onion sandwich 43
cheese and pineapple salad 55
cheese and salami croissant 38
cheese and sweetcorn soup 61
croque monsieur 42
easy strawberry cheesecake 185
macaroni cheese 67
mock cheese soufflé 78
roasted peppers with Halloumi 76
sausage burgers with cheese 135
simple cheese and bacon pasta 146
Swiss cheese and pineapple (toast) 44
Swiss cheese and potato bake 70
tomato soup with mozzarella 30
tuna, cheese and sweetcorn 159
tuna and cream cheese paté 47
tuna salad with garlic and cheese 156
chick pea pasta 82
chicken
baked chicken in tomato sauce 102
chicken and coconut masala 100
chicken and corn chowder 94
chicken and mushroom risotto 97
chicken and pesto baguette 56
chicken and vegetable stir-fry 104
curried chicken mayonnaise 107
curried chicken and potato salad 108
cutting into portions 95
grilled chicken with garlic 103
honey and lemon chicken 96
lightly spiced chicken casserole 100
one-step roast chicken 106
quick chicken chow mein 99
tandoori chicken 95
Thai green chicken curry 105
chilli con carne 117
chilli tacos in minutes 126
chips, preparing 16
chocolate mousse, almost instant 178
chocolate sauce
banana split and chocolate sauce 182
ice cream and chocolate sauces 174
chopping, defined 19

chow mein, quick chicken 99
chowder
cheese and sweetcorn chowder 61
chicken and corn chowder 94
coconut
chewy fruit and coconut bars 167
chicken and coconut masala 100
corned beef
corned beef fritters 121
corned beef pan hash 127
cottage pie, vegetable 69
courgettes, cooking technique 17
couscous with spiced lamb 131
croissant, cheese and salami 38
croque monsieur 42
crunch bars, no-bake 169
cupboard contents, basics 13
curry
chicken and coconut masala 100
curried bean and rice salad 88
curried chicken mayonnaise 107
curried chicken and potato salad 108
curried vegetable soup 64
Keema curry and rice 119
lightly spiced chicken casserole 100
tandoori chicken 95
Thai fish curry 151
Thai green chicken curry 105

definitions 19–20
dhal 77
dicing, defined 19

eggs
chilli vegetables with baked eggs 68
cooking techniques 15
egg foo yung with rice 153
great British fry-up 145
mock cheese soufflé 78
piperade 85
savoury egg rice 72
separating 20
see also omelettes
equipment, checklist 11

fish
  easy fish pâté 54
  fish creole 162
  fish finger and mayonnaise 31
  fish and potato fry 155
  fish in tomato and pepper sauce 154
  nutrition 9
  one-pot kedgeree 158
  quick fish pot 150
  Thai fish curry 151
  types of 149
  see also specific fish dishes
flameproof, defined 18, 19
flapjacks
  banana sultana flapjacks 171
  Mum's flapjacks 170
folding, defined 19
food
  basics 13–14
  hygiene 22
  storage 21–2
frankfurters
  hot chilli dogs 39
  sauerkraut with frankfurters 140
French toast 48
  cinnamon French toast 168
fridge, basics checklist 14
fried eggs 15
fritters
  corn fritters with peanut sauce 83
  corned beef fritters 121
frozen vegetables 17
fruit and coconut bars, chewy 167
fruit crumble, no-effort 183
fruit portions 9
fry-up, great British 145

grating, defined 19
Greek-style roast lamb 129
Greek-style salad 91
green beans, omelette with 45
green vegetables 17

ham
  broccoli with ham and cheese 128
  cheese and ham pancakes 143
  grilled ham with pineapple 142
  penne with ham and peas 141
  toasted ham and cheese sandwich 42
hash, corned beef pan 127
herb and salami garlic bread 51
herbs, fresh 19
honey and lemon chicken 96
hot chilli dogs 39
hygiene 21–2

ice cream and chocolate sauces 174

jacket-baked potatoes 16
  stuffed jacket potatoes 26

kebabs, sheesh 130
kedgeree, one-pot 158
kidneys, devilled, with rice 125
kitchen
  equipment, checklist 11
  hygiene 21–2
kneading, defined 19

lamb
  couscous with spiced lamb 131
  Greek-style roast lamb 129
  sheesh kebabs 130
lasagne al forno 116
lemon pie 179
lemon sauce, bananas and hot 181
lentils
  dhal 77
  lentil and vegetable soup 60
liver, peppered, with carrot mash 124

macaroni
  macaroni cheese 67
  salmon macaroni 160
mackerel
  mustard mackerel 152
  smoked mackerel bagels 53

market stalls 9
mashing
    defined 19–20
    peppered liver with carrot mash 124
    potatoes 16
measures, recipe 23
meat
    cuts 9
    meat loaf 113
minced beef *see* beef
minestrone 65
mousse, almost instant chocolate 178
mushrooms
    cheese and mushroom wedges 75
    chicken and mushroom risotto 97
    mushroom and nut pilaf 74
    spiced mushrooms 50

naan bread wedges, stuffed 37
nachos 32
nuts
    corn fritters with peanut sauce 83
    mushroom and nut pilaf 74
    peanut soup 66

omelettes
    cheese and mushroom wedges 75
    mushroom omelette baguette 41
    omelette with green beans 45
    tortilla 84
onions
    brown onion soup 63
    cheese and onion pitta bread 49
    cheese and onion sandwich 43
    slicing 20
oven-baked rice 18
ovenproof, defined 18, 19, 20

pancakes, cheese and ham 143
paring, defined 20
pasta
    chick pea pasta 82
    cooking technique 18
    pasta with corn and spinach 81

quick beef pasta 114
sauces 27
simple cheese and bacon pasta 146
see also specific types
pastrami on rye, hot 52
pâté
    easy fish 54
    tuna and cream cheese 47
peanut soup 66
peas
    pease pudding 37
    penne with ham and peas 141
penne with ham and peas 141
peppers with Halloumi, roasted 76
pilaf
    mushroom and nut pilaf 74
    quick smoked sausage pilaf 139
pineapple
    cheese and pineapple salad 55
    grilled ham with pineapple 142
    pineapple pudding 177
piperade 85
pitta bread
    cheese and onion pitta bread 49
    pitta pockets 35
    tzatziki with pittas 57
pizza, quick pan 87
poached eggs 15
pork
    pork and noodle stir-fry 134
    pork steaks with cabbage 132
    sweet and sour pork slices 133
potatoes
    cooking techniques 15–17
    curried chicken and potato salad 108
    fish and potato fry 155
    hot potato and bacon salad 147
    potato moussaka 122
    rich mince with new potatoes 118
    salmon and potato salad 161
    spicy potato cakes 33
    stuffed jacket potatoes 26
    Swiss cheese and potato bake 70
prawn risotto 163

protein 9

quesadillas 36

ratatouille, one-step 86
recipe measures 23
rhubarb and custard charlotte 176
rice
    banana rice pudding layer 175
    chicken and mushroom risotto 97
    cooking techniques 17–18
    curried bean and rice salad 88
    devilled kidneys with rice 125
    egg foo yung with rice 153
    fish creole 162
    Keema curry and rice 119
    mushroom and nut pilaf 74
    prawn risotto 163
    quick smoked sausage pilaf 139
    sauces 28
    savoury egg rice 72
    sticky barbecue bangers and rice 136
    vegetable risotto 73
roasting
    Greek-style roast lamb 129
    one-step roast chicken 106
    potatoes 16
    root vegetables 17
rolling, defined 20
root vegetables 17

salads
    cheese and pineapple salad 55
    curried bean and rice salad 88
    curried chicken and potato salad 108
    Greek-style salad 91
    hot potato and bacon salad 147
    salmon and potato salad 161
    sausage salad with croûtons 138
    tuna salad with garlic and cheese 156
salami
    cheese and salami croissant 38
    herb and salami garlic bread 51

salmon
    salmon macaroni 160
    salmon and potato salad 161
salsa 32
sardines
    easy fish pâté
sauerkraut with frankfurters 140
sausages
    great British fry-up 145
    quick smoked sausage pilaf 139
    sausage burgers with cheese 135
    sausage salad with croûtons 138
    sticky barbecue bangers and rice 136
    toad in the hole 137
    types 9
sautéed potatoes 16–17
savoury egg rice 72
scrambled eggs 15
seafood, prawn risotto 163
sheesh kebabs 130
shopping basics 13–14
slicing, onions 20
smoked mackerel bagels 53
snacks 167–71
soup
    brown onion soup 63
    cheese and sweetcorn soup 61
    curried vegetable soup 64
    double tomato and bean soup 62
    lentil and vegetable soup 60
    minestrone 65
    peanut soup 66
    thick mixed vegetable soup 29
    tomato soup with mozzarella 30
    see also chowder
spaghetti
    cooking technique 18
    spaghetti bolognese 115
    spaghetti carbonara 144
    spaghetti with pesto 90
    spaghetti with tomato sauce 71
spinach, pasta with corn and 81
starchy food 9
steak, piquant pan-fried 123

steaming
    green vegetables 17
    rice 18
stir-fry
    black bean vegetable stir-fry 89
    chicken and vegetable stir-fry 104
    cooking technique 17
    pork and noodle stir-fry 134
storing food 21–2
strawberry cheesecake, easy 185
supermarkets 9
sweet snacks 167–71
sweet and sour pork slices 133
sweetcorn
    cheese and sweetcorn soup 61
    chicken and corn chowder 94
    corn fritters with peanut sauce 83
    pasta with corn and spinach 81
    tuna, cheese and sweetcorn 159
Swiss cheese *see under* cheese

tandoori chicken 95
terminology 19–20
Thai fish curry 151
Thai green chicken curry 105
toad in the hole 137
toast
    cinnamon French toast 168
    French toast 48
    hot pastrami on rye 52
    Swiss cheese and pineapple 44
    toasted ham and cheese sandwich 42
tomatoes
    baked chicken in tomato sauce 102
    double tomato and bean soup 62
    fish in tomato and pepper sauce 154
    great British fry-up 145
    spaghetti with tomato sauce 71

tomato soup with mozzarella 30
tortilla
    chips 32
    flour 36
    Spanish omelette 84
tuna
    creamy tuna dip 46
    tuna, cheese and sweetcorn 159
    tuna and chilli mayo wraps 40
    tuna and cream cheese paté 47
    tuna mornay 157
    tuna salad with garlic and cheese 156
turkey
    crunchy turkey steaks 98
    turkey stroganoff 109
tzatziki with pittas 57

utensils, cooking 11

vegetables
    black bean vegetable stir-fry 89
    chicken and vegetable stir-fry 104
    chilli vegetables with baked eggs 68
    curried vegetable soup 64
    frozen 17
    green 17
    lentil and vegetable soup 60
    one-step ratatouille 86
    portions 9
    root 17
    stir-fried 17
    thick mixed vegetable soup 29
    vegetable cottage pie 69
    vegetable risotto 73
    see also specific vegetables 73

whipping/whisking, defined 20
wraps, tuna and chilli mayo 40